A Gift for

_____

Presented by

_____

OH, SAY
DID YOU KNOW?

OH, SAY
DID YOU KNOW?

The Secret History
of America's Famous Figures,
Fads, Innovations & Emblems,
from Ben Franklin's Turkey
to Obama's BlackBerry

Fred DuBose & Martha Hailey

The Reader's Digest Association, Inc.
Pleasantville, NY/Montreal/London

U.S. Project Editor: Kim Casey
Copy Editor: Jen Graham
Indexer: Nan Badgett
Project Designer: Elizabeth Tunnicliffe
Senior Art Director: George McKeon
Executive Editor, Trade Publishing: Dolores York
Manufacturing Manager: Elizabeth Dinda
Associate Publisher: Rosanne McManus
President and Publisher, Trade Publishing: Harold Clarke

Library of Congress Cataloging-in-Publication Data
DuBose, Fred.
Oh say, did you know? : the secret history of America's famous figures, fads, innovations &
emblems from Ben Franklin's turkey to Obama's blackberry / Fred DuBose & Martha Hailey.
p. cm.
ISBN 978-1-60652-035-2
1. United States--History--Anecdotes. 2. United States--Social life and customs--
Anecdotes. 3. United States--Biography--Anecdotes. 4. National characteristics, American--
Anecdotes. I. DuBose, Martha Hailey. II. Title.
E178.6.D79 2009
973--dc22

2009019425

We are committed to both the quality of our products and the service we provide to
our customers. We value your comments, so please feel free to contact us:
The Reader's Digest Association, Inc., Adult Trade Publishing, Pleasantville, NY 10570-7000.

For more Reader's Digest products and information, visit our website:
www.rd.com (in the United States)
www.rd.ca (in Canada)
www.readersdigest.com (in the UK)

Printed in the United States of America

1 3 5 7 9 10 8 6 4 2

Acknowledgments

The authors give special thanks to John H. Barcroft, Ph.D., for sharing his original
ideas and seasoned eye. Others who deserve our gratitude are John Bence, Anthony
Cekay, Juleigh Clark, Pat Courtney, Joseph DeBusk, Polly DuBose, Paul Fahle, Adam
Gustafson, Anne Haines, Kristin Hastings, David and Ginger Hildebrand, Sharon
Jarvis, Richard Johnson, Alfred Kennedy, Grahame Long, Sarah Morin, Brian
Peterson, Babette Samuels, Jon Shestakofsky, Kent Stephens, Margaret Thomas, Kate
Tomassi, Kimberly Toon, Margaret Tremper, and Jennifer Yeadon.

An investment in knowledge always pays the best interest.

— **Benjamin Franklin**

Contents

Introduction
10

Maypoles to Midnight Rides: Colonial America 12

CARVING OUT THE COLONIES

*English settlement started at Jamestown and spread up and down the
eastern seaboard. As major European powers vied for control, ordinary
people broke ground and built communities.*

13

THE ROAD TO INDEPENDENCE

*Bristling under British rule, the colonists found leaders in the men we
now call the Founding Fathers and courage among countless farmers,
tradespeople, homemakers, slaves, and servants.*

29

A REVOLUTION LIKE NO OTHER

*Although many colonists had no desire to separate from England, the
forces of freedom prevailed, and the newly declared and ill-prepared
United States of America went to war.*

34

Start-Up to Superpower:
Our Government and Growth 42

A ROCKY START

*The new United States had a Constitution, president, Congress, and
little else. Nothing like this self-governing republic had ever been tried
before, and the nation struggled to define itself.*

43

BOOM, BUST, BOOM YEARS

*From the Gilded Age through the Great Depression and World War II,
the American Dream took a wild roller-coaster ride of thrilling high
points and devastating plunges.*

60

MODERN TIMES

*After World War II we weathered the cold war, became the world's only
superpower, and saw the founders' ideals realized with the election of the
nation's first African American president.*

71

Sailing Ships to Space Stations:
Our Industry and Innovations 78

INDUSTRY'S SECOND WAVE

*In England the arrival of the steam engine (1776) started the Industrial
Revolution, and a second wave soon began to swell across the pond.*

79

THE WORLD OF WORK

*From colonial days on, Americans toiled as farm workers, tradespeople, or
merchants—but the nature of labor of any stripe was in for a big change.*

84

ON THE FARM

*The American economy rode almost wholly on the backs of farmers until
the Second Industrial Revolution sowed the seeds of mechanized agriculture.*

87

ECONOMIC UPS AND DOWNS

*Our economy has seen good times and bad, a force that alternately
gained steam and sputtered after we began trading stocks in 1792.*

91

THEY, TOO, MADE THEIR MARK

*Thomas Edison, Alexander Graham Bell, and their famous counterparts tend
to overshadow a number of other innovators who deserve a place in history.*

97

THE THIRD WAVE

The Third Industrial Revolution was a tidal wave that started with the U.S. space program and swept on to the IT Revolution.

102

Buildings to Burials: Our Daily Lives 106

HOME AND HEARTH

To make America their home, new arrivals had to build houses and neighborhoods. Their earliest shelters were barely habitable, but the migrants learned to make do and move forward.

107

MARRYING AND BREAKING UP

Colonial Americans courted quickly, married young, and stayed hitched until death did them part. That began to change in the 1800s, thanks in part to some high-profile scandals.

112

RAISING FAMILIES

Early American families functioned like small industries. Everyone worked together. But the rise of the middle class brought a separation of domestic responsibilities.

116

THE FOOD ON OUR TABLES

The idea that food could be pleasurable was a hard sell in early America. Then new technologies and the introduction of variety in the daily diet changed tastes.

120

THE CLOTHES ON OUR BACKS

The early colonists didn't care how they looked, but as soon as Americans started making money, they expanded their wardrobe and dress became fashionable.

126

SICKNESS AND DEATH

Battling illness and injury has been a constant theme in our history, and our funeral customs have changed over time.

132

Virginia Reels to Video Games: Our Entertainments and Pastimes 138

ALL TOGETHER NOW

In our earliest days taverns were the primary gathering places for men, but males and females alike took part in "frolics," communal house and barn raisings, and picnics.

139

SONG AND DANCE

We put our own stamp on music and dance from the mother countries, and in doing so made a joyful —and sometimes mournful—noise.

142

GAMES, GAMES, GAMES

Many of our games and sports testify to the knack our ancestors had for taking the traditions of the Old World and turning them into something new.

146

READING MATTER

By the late 1700s the majority of Americans were literate, and there was no shortage of books and publications to keep them occupied.

152

STAGE AND SCREEN

In the 19th century we finally created our own theatrical traditions. In the next century we introduced the world to an art form, the likes of which it had never seen before: the Hollywood movie.

155

RADIO AND TV

Radio was one of the miracles of the Jazz Age—but as entertainer Al Jolson worded it, Americans of the 1920s "ain't seen nothin' yet!"

161

ASSORTED AMUSEMENTS

Fun parks and showmen like P. T. Barnum did much to amuse us, and a late-1800s flowering of museum-going threw enlightenment into the mix.

165

Index

170

Introduction

WHO KNEW?

The deeper we dig into the rich soil of American history, the more surprising, incredible, or downright strange are the stories that crop up. Some important people and happenings never made it into the history books, and many that did were eventually forgotten. And even the familiar whos, whats, and whens of our past can reveal a hidden side once you scratch the surface.

Some examples of what you'll find in this book:

- Isaac Singer of sewing machine fame lived a life straight out of a novel—one that leaned toward pulp fiction. (Page 101)
- In 1872 a raging epizootic (epidemic in animals) sickened virtually all of the horses in the United States, leaving the economy in ruins. (Page 134)
- Author and activist Lydia Maria Child was so accomplished she should practically be on our money, yet she's barely remembered. (Page 152)
- The 1904 Olympics in St. Louis was pretty much one big mess during its ten-week run, but a rather endearing mess. (Page 148)

Oh, Say Did You Know? brings you more than 200 such stories, broken down into five chapters touching on the colonial period, the birth pangs and growth of a new nation, our industries and innovations, our changing customs, and our pastimes. Special features and sidebars throw light on everything from unexpected national emblems to the financial panics that preceded the Great Depression. "Didn't Happen!" sidebars set a number of longstanding misconceptions straight, while "Our Native Tongue" sidebars reveal how much color American speech has brought to the English language.

GET SMART

This little book is a great big springboard for your own forays into American history. A name, an event, a custom may pique your curiosity and send you to a library or the Internet to learn more. Who could fail to be fascinated by financier J. P. Morgan, who had a thing for astrology and belonged to a 12-man secret society of fellow believers? Or Alva Vanderbilt, who forced her daughter into a loveless marriage to an English duke and staged what the *New York Times* called "the most magnificent [wedding] ever celebrated in this country"? Or Nicholas Trist, who was sent by President Polk to negotiate a peace treaty with Mexico, succeeded, and was promptly fired?

Likewise, many clashes and coincidences got lost in the shuffle as time marched on. Patriots and loyalists fought an actual battle against each other at Kings Mountain in South Carolina a year before we won our independence. Two World War I ambulance drivers thrown together as bunkmates went their separate ways after the war and founded two of the world's largest corporations.

Stories like these are intriguing in their own right, but we hope they'll also put you on your own path of discovery. The more you read and investigate, the more likely you are to start assembling the bits and pieces of our nation's history into one big, fascinating whole—an outsize reward from a book of only 176 pages.

11

Maypoles to Midnight Rides

Colonial America

It began with immigrants. The first mass migration came from Asia many centuries before the continent had a name. The second, from Europe, laid the foundations of the United States. The European settlers lived and governed themselves by the customs, rules, and faiths of their efforts to adapt to each other and to strange, new conditions.

CARVING OUT THE COLONIES

ENGLISH SETTLEMENT STARTED AT JAMESTOWN AND SPREAD
UP AND DOWN THE EASTERN SEABOARD. AS MAJOR EUROPEAN
POWERS VIED FOR CONTROL, ORDINARY PEOPLE BROKE GROUND
AND BUILT COMMUNITIES.

FAITH AND PROFIT

English settlers came to America for many reasons, including the
desire to escape religious persecution and practice their own faiths
without restraint. But the first British colonies were set up as purely
commercial ventures. In 1606 English merchants received a charter
from King James I, incorporating the Virginia Company of Plymouth
(New England) and the Virginia Company of London (the Southern colonies). In exchange for the king's largesse, investors recruited
settlers, paid for their passage, and financed settlements.

In return, the colonists were expected to turn all their profits
back to the private companies for a period of seven years. Similar companies backed Dutch and French colonies. With very few
exceptions, the shareholders who expected to profit from these early
ventures never set foot on American shores.

WHAT WERE THEY THINKING?

Passenger lists from the ships that carried the earliest settlers (1606–
1609) to Jamestown reveal a lot about how little was known about
survival in the New World. The first ships listed 29 "gentlemen" and
just 13 laborers.

The next arrivals included 28 gents and 21 laborers.

A third wave brought more supplies as well as 26 gentlemen, 11 laborers, and the colony's first women—the wife of a gentleman and her maid.

Also on board the ships were artisans with practical skills: carpenters, masons and bricklayers, and a blacksmith. But it's difficult to account for the presence of a jeweler, a perfumer, and a tobacco-pipe maker.

Tossed in a Shakespearean Tempest

Seven supply ships set out for Virginia in June 1609. It was the maiden voyage of the London Company's flagship *Sea Venture,* the first British merchant vessel designed to transport passengers. Battered for days by a hurricane, the fleet was scattered, and construction flaws caused the *Sea Venture* to leak badly. Spotting land, Company Admiral Sir George Somers deliberately steered the ship onto the reefs, enabling his crew and passengers to escape. Stranded on a deserted island, the survivors built two boats and finally reached Jamestown nine months later.

Based on the shipwreck, England laid claim to Bermuda, which was incorporated into the London Company's charter. A later account by *Sea Venture* survivor William Strachey reached England and became the inspiration for William Shakespeare's final play, *The Tempest.*

"TOBACCO BRIDES"

The Virginia colony's first sizable influx of English women included many who indentured themselves and were auctioned to eager settlers for 120 pounds of tobacco; some who paid their own way; and a few who chose the New World as the alternative to an English prison. All had their pick of marriage partners.

A few prospered, like Temperance Flowerdew, who married two colonial governors. Most didn't do quite so well but took advantage of unique opportunities to own land and run businesses. Mortality in the Chesapeake Bay region was very high (nearly two-thirds of the first 6,000 settlers were dead by 1625), and due to the death of a partner, the average marriage lasted only seven years. Wives tended to outlast their husbands because so many marriages were May-December affairs. Jamestown's first wedding was between a 14-year-old servant girl and a laborer twice her age.

JAMESTOWN'S STRICT DISCIPLINARIAN

Sir Thomas Dale landed in Jamestown in 1611, soon after the "Starving Time" that nearly wiped out the settlement. Sent at the request of the London Company to rescue their investment, he accomplished the task by authoring laws, known as Dale's Code, and imposing what amounted to martial law.

The Jamestown colonists clearly resented Dale's harsh methods, but historians agree that without his discipline the colony would have collapsed. A couple of months later, Dale applied the same relentless drive to construction of a fortified town, Henricus, 30 miles up the James River. Henricus was intended to remove colonists from the malarial swamps around Jamestown and also serve notice on Spain, which claimed much of North America but had done little to encourage colonization.

During a second sojourn as deputy governor of Virginia, Dale promoted settlement of the Eastern Shore of Chesapeake Bay, negotiated with the Powhatan tribe, and engineered the marriage of Pocahontas, daughter of the Powhatan chief, to John Rolfe.

A WONDERFUL WORLD OF WOOD

Early settlers were astounded by the woods and forests they encountered, because England by this time had been largely cleared of its native timber. Trees that had to be cut for agricultural fields provided the colonists with a ready-made commodity for trade.

Well before decent roads were built, logs were floated down the new country's vast coastal system of rivers and streams to waiting ships. The Old World was a huge and hungry market for logs and lumber, especially for shipbuilding and construction, so wood in every form quickly became one of the colonists' most successful economic ventures.

THIS WOMAN MEANT BUSINESS

When Margaret Brent, her sister, and her brother arrived in Maryland in 1636, they immediately set to work. Under the authority of Lord Baltimore himself, the Brent women owned their own property, which they named Sisters' Freehold, and Margaret started a business lending money to new settlers.

No shrinking violet, Margaret sued whenever borrowers didn't pay their debts, argued her court cases herself, and usually won. In 1648 she stood before the Maryland Assembly and demanded two votes in the legislative body—one for herself and the other as executor of the estate of the recently deceased colonial governor, Leonard Calvert. She lost that fight but is remembered as America's first female lawyer for her legal skills and her boldness.

SEPARATISTS AND IDEALISTS AT ODDS

The Protestant Pilgrims who founded the Plymouth colony in 1620 were Separatists. But this wasn't the true for the Puritan Congregationalists who set up the Massachusetts Bay colony in 1630. Both groups were Puritans and held the same core beliefs, but they differed on what to do about the Church of England.

Pilgrims chose to leave Anglicanism behind entirely. Congregationalists sought to cleanse the English church of its Roman Catholic rituals and hierarchies and to create an ideal community of self-governing believers in America as a model for their English brethren.

One fellow who got caught in the theological crossfire was Roger Williams. First a Congregationalist and then a Separatist, Williams was finally run out of Massachusetts altogether for his radical ideas about religious freedom. He moved on to establish Rhode Island, the most religiously tolerant of all the colonies.

A *Mayflower* Mystery

Dorothy May and William Bradford married when she was 16 and lived in Leyden—a Dutch haven for English Separatists—before striking out for the New World in 1620. After a stormy 65-day voyage to what the Pilgrims hoped would be Virginia, the *Mayflower* anchored off Cape Cod, Massachusetts. Some weeks later, while William and a party of men were ashore, Dorothy went overboard and drowned.

Did she fall or jump? Suicide was not so uncommon among the early colonists. Bereft of her toddler son (left behind in Leyden) and drained by the journey, cold weather, three deaths aboard the ship, and perhaps fearing her husband would never return, the 23-year-old Dorothy might have had enough. The absence of any details in the ship's log and Bradford's journals raises suspicions, and to this day, no one knows if Dorothy's body was ever recovered, buried, or prayed over.

PESTERING THE PILGRIMS

Want to annoy a Pilgrim? Raise an 80-foot Maypole, brew "a barrell of excellent beer," throw a loud party, and invite the local American Indians. That and other antics earned Thomas Morton— Anglican, lawyer, and one of the owner-founders of Ma-re (Merry) Mount plantation in Massachusetts—the everlasting enmity of nearby Plymouth.

The Ma-re Mount settlers established themselves within ear-shot of the Pilgrims in 1622. When the group's leader left, Morton took charge, freed the indentured servants, and with the help of the

Indians, whom Morton greatly admired, began a successful trade exchanging guns for beaver fur.

To William Bradford, the plantation was "a School of Atheism" and Morton its "Lord of Misrule." Morton's refusal to reject the Anglican *Book of Common Prayer* and his trading of guns with the nearby tribes seem to have been the main sources of Puritan anger, leading to harassment, arrests, and Morton's deportation to England. Eventually Morton returned, was jailed for a year, and lived out his life in the wilderness.

Morton is remembered not just for his defiance but also for his intense, joyful love of the new continent. "It was Paradise," he wrote, ". . . Nature's Master-peece." Later American writers, including Nathaniel Hawthorne, featured Morton in stories, plays, and an opera.

"First, Kill All the Lawyers"

Remembering their experiences under the English legal system, the colonists didn't trust lawyers. The Massachusetts Bay Bodie of Liberties (1641) forbade payments to anyone representing another in court. Virginia literally threw out all its lawyers in 1658 and didn't allow them back for 28 years.

Legal education in our modern sense didn't exist, and most colonists represented themselves before judges who were only marginally less ignorant of legal technicalities. But this wasn't necessarily a bad thing. By relying on frontier justice, the colonists didn't import the hierarchical, class-ridden British system. They simply taught themselves enough law for everyday transactions, trusted the common sense of judges and juries, and gradually constructed a practical justice system more egalitarian than any in Europe.

Our early lawyers, including those who wrote the Constitution, were mostly self-taught. In 1777 the first "Professorship of Law" was introduced at Yale University. It wasn't until Rutherford B. Hayes was elected that a president had a law degree (Harvard, class of 1845). Washington, D.C. may be awash in lawyers now, but a streak of colonial mistrust survives: Of our 13 presidents since 1934, only Nixon, Ford, Clinton, and Obama graduated from law school.

THE GOODWIFE REBEL OF BOSTON

Anne Hutchinson and her family arrived in the Massachusetts colony in 1634. Hutchinson, the daughter of a clergyman and well educated in theology, openly espoused her religious belief that knowledge of a person's ultimate destiny was between the individual and God and was not to be interpreted by clergymen. Her discussions brought followers to her door and the wrath of the colonial leaders down on her head.

There's no evidence Hutchinson intended to be a rabble-rouser, but within a year she was accused of sedition. Records of her trial indicate that even her accusers weren't sure if she had committed any real crime, other than expressing her own version of Puritanism. But that was enough for the powers that be. Hutchinson was convicted, held under house arrest, and finally expelled from the colony.

WAR WITH "KING PHILIP"

The Puritans got along with the indigenous peoples while the friendship was advantageous. But by the mid-1600s, the settlers needed more land, and the American Indian tribes of New England were in the way. By 1675 all pretense of cooperation had vanished, and the Indians and the settlers were at war. The fighting consisted primarily of deadly raids and vicious retaliations, with heavy losses on both sides.

The Narragansett tribes were virtually wiped out, but the American Indians didn't relent until the Wampanoag chief Metacom ("King Philip" to the English) was killed in August 1676. Their morale broken, most of the surviving tribespeople fled the region.

A peace treaty signed in 1678 finally ended the most brutal conflict in colonial New England history. As a reminder of the costly victory, Metacom's severed head was kept on public display in Plymouth for another quarter century.

WEETAMO, WARRIOR PRINCESS

The daughter of the chief of the Pocasset tribe, Weetamo (c. 1640–1676), was groomed, as a son would have been, to succeed her father. In King Philip's War, Weetamo is said to have been a strong and brave leader of her warriors. She drowned in the Taunton River while attempting to escape a colonial ambush, and her recovered body suffered the same degradation as Metacom's.

PURITAN THOU-SHALT-NOTS

The first Puritan settlers believed that all the laws they needed were in the Bible, but in real life this faith caused some mind-bending logic in the early days. For example, Scripture required that adulterers be stoned to death; this struck even stern Puritans as too severe, especially when the offenders were community leaders or clergymen.

After some early excesses, the Puritans relied primarily on punishment by public humiliation—confinement to the stocks, lashings, fines, forms of house arrest and shunning, and in extreme cases, banishment. Tarring and feathering was generally reserved for troublesome outsiders. Murder, rape, sodomy, witchcraft, or insurrection warranted death, and the early Puritans had some grisly ways of dispatching their worst felons.

Everyday infractions included wearing a touch of lace or the wrong size dress sleeves, long hair on men, kissing one's spouse in public, gossiping maliciously, and missing church. Giving birth on a Sunday was punishable by a hefty fine because it was taken as proof that a couple had violated the Sabbath nine months earlier.

WHAT'S BLUE ABOUT "BLUE LAWS"?

Puritans were adamant about the Fourth Commandment, reserving Sundays for worship, Bible reading, spiritual contemplation, and little else. Church attendance was compulsory. Cooking, gardening, hunting, playing, and riding were prohibited. No one was immune. In 1789 newly elected President George Washington, while traveling to New York, was detained by local Connecticut authorities for riding on the Sabbath.

Why "blue"? It's not, as the myth goes, because colonial laws were printed on blue paper or in books with blue covers. The first written use of the term is attributed to the Reverend Samuel Peters, a wealthy Anglican colonist and British loyalist, who fled to London during the Revolution. In England at the time, "blue" meant characterized by rigid moral standards—in other words, Puritanical.

Off with Their Hats

Puritans and Quakers got along like cats and dogs. The first Quakers to arrive in America were refugees from the West Indies, and their missionary zeal quickly had them banned from the Massachusetts colonies. But the Quakers came anyway to preach their version of Protestantism, precipitating a period (1656–1665) of persecutions, imprisonments—many Quaker men were thrown into jail simply for refusing to remove their hats when in church or court—and public executions that presaged the Salem Witch Trials.

Mary Dyer, the best-known Quaker dissenter, had to work hard to achieve the martyrdom she and other Quakers desperately wanted. Saved at the last minute as she stood on a Boston gallows (her two male companions were hanged), Dyer was banished to Rhode Island. Two years later, in 1660, the persistent Mrs. Dyer was back in Boston again—hanging by the neck from a Puritan rope.

SEX AND THE MARRIED PURITAN

Despite their uptight image, the Puritans had a strong sensual side and believed that as a gift from God, sex should be enjoyed by both participants, as long as they were married. Adultery was anathema; whenever a secret liaison was discovered, both sinners were punished—women more harshly than men. Remember *The Scarlet Letter*?

Premarital sex between engaged people became a thorny problem toward the end of the 1600s—reflected in the increasing number of healthy "seven-month babies" born to upright Puritan couples. Studies of marriage and birth records from all the colonies indicate that at least 20 to 30 percent of colonial brides were pregnant on their wedding day.

Rape, defined as nonconsensual sex with a girl under age 10, became a capital offense in Massachusetts after a messy 1642 case.

THE QUAKER'S MOVER AND SHAKER

British Admiral Sir William Penn Sr. raised his son to be a gentleman. William Penn Jr. attended Oxford, completed his studies in France, and trained in law at Lincoln's Inn in London. But young Penn sorely tested his father's patience. Attracted to the humanistic faith of the Quakers, he became an outspoken convert at a time when simply attending a Quaker meeting was illegal.

Penn was jailed numerous times and might have languished in prison for years, as many English Quakers did, but he was saved by his father's close relationships with the Stuart kings. In 1670 Penn directly challenged Britain's Conventicle Act—which prohibited gatherings by non-Anglican religious groups. He was arrested once again and argued a landmark court case that established the principle that juries could not be intimidated by the authorities or punished for their verdicts.

Penn's lengthy legal battle, combined with travels in religiously tolerant Holland and Germany, convinced him to use his father's connections to get a piece of the New World for Quakers and others seeking freedom from religious persecution. In 1681 Charles II of England granted Penn a charter for Pennsylvania, named by the king to honor Admiral Penn.

CLASS WARFARE IN VIRGINIA

Bacon's Rebellion is often passed over in history class because the motives for the 1676 uprising—pitting Virginia frontier farmers, slaves, and indentured servants against the elitist coastal planters and Governor William Berkeley—are myriad and confusing. Led by the charismatic Nathaniel Bacon, a newly arrived English gentleman, farmers to the west rose up to protest a lack of royal protection from American Indian attacks and looming tax increases at a time when tobacco sales were slumping.

The rebellion failed when Bacon suddenly died, probably of dysentery. Not soon enough, however, to prevent the murders of a number of innocent Indians and the burning of Jamestown. Berkeley fled to England, and order was restored when 23 of Bacon's rebellious farmers were tried and hanged, concluding America's first violent revolt against British rule.

THE TROUBLE WITH TOBACCO

Tobacco was one of the Southern colonies' early cash crops, but it was not the easiest to produce. As colonial farmers soon learned, tobacco cultivation was a major pain. From seeding through drying and curing, tobacco required almost a year of devoted attention. Producing a good crop included handpicking pests off tender plants and endless pruning—time usually bought at the expense of cultivating easier-to-grow corn and grains.

Tobacco also depleted the soil after two or three seasons, requiring constant clearing of new fields. It wasn't until the introduction of machine-rolled cigarettes in the 1800s that tobacco began to live up to its full moneymaking potential (see also Our First Cash Crop, page 87.)

DIDN'T HAPPEN!

A Cross-Dressing Governor?

A grand portrait of Edward Hyde, Lord Cornbury, royal governor of New York and New Jersey (1701–1709), shows him with a lady's coiffure and lace cap, dressed in women's clothing, and dangling a fan from delicate fingers. But is the dignified painted lady really Cornbury in drag or the concoction of his colonial enemies? Recent investigation has turned up no firsthand evidence that the governor, who was the nephew of King James II and the ardent supporter of his cousins Queens Mary and Anne, was anything more than the victim of political dirty tricks.

PAINTING THE COLONIES

Limners were itinerant artists, mostly untrained, who traveled the colonies painting anything people were willing to pay for, such as clock faces, tavern signs, and fire screens. With the rise of the merchant class in the 1700s, limners were also commissioned to render family portraits. Although they are valuable now for their age and quaintness, these early portraits are hardly high art. Many limners painted bodies in advance and simply filled in faces and some personal details for their paying clients.

Often the faces of whole families had a disturbing, clonelike sameness, and small children, even babies, were depicted with adult-size heads. Although not high art, the surviving works of anonymous limners do provide us with a visual record of middle-class lifestyles, family customs, and colonial aspirations.

GEORGIA ON HIS MIND

Georgia, the last of the British colonies to be chartered (1732) and the only one funded by the British Parliament, was the dream of soldier and social reformer James Oglethorpe. He envisioned a place populated by England's "worthy poor," meaning imprisoned debtors—but in the end, not a single debtor was among the first settlers. The colony's charter was unique in guaranteeing its citizens the rights of Englishmen and prohibiting slavery.

Georgia prospered under Oglethorpe's hands-on leadership. Among his achievements were his plan for the city of Savannah, which he laid out in a pattern that excluded class distinctions among property holders, his insistence on opening the colony to religious minorities, and his policies respecting American Indian land rights and customs.

After his return to England in 1743, Oglethorpe was eased out of the colony's governing board, and many of his reforms, including the prohibition of slavery, were abandoned. But he did live to see his colony become independent. A few weeks before his death in 1885, the old general expressed his "great esteem and regard" for the new nation to Ambassador John Adams.

THE WAR OF JENKINS'S EAR

Although it was barely a blip on the radar of colonial history, the Spain-versus-England conflict known as the War of Jenkins's Ear (named for a British sea captain who claimed to have lost an ear to a Spanish privateer) spilled over briefly into Georgia.

In 1734 General James Oglethorpe and his English rangers, after failing to seize St. Augustine, defeated Spanish invaders in the Battle of Bloody Marsh (St. Simon's Island). This victory effectively established the border between the Georgia colony and Spanish-controlled Florida.

THOSE WORLDLY DUTCH

The Dutch were populating and profiting from North America long before England began to take an interest. As the world's leading sea power for much of the 1500s, the freewheeling and tolerant Dutch gained control of the resource-rich Hudson River and established outposts there, including the key port of New Amsterdam (New York).

Endless conflict with other European powers wore the early settlers down, and in 1664, in an act that still defies explanation, the Dutch governor surrendered the prosperous colony, without any resistance, to the Duke of York's naval fleet. The remaining Dutch adapted to the change of allegiance without too much rancor, and their influence is still evident in our most cosmopolitan city.

OUR NATIVE TONGUE

The Dutch Origin of "Yankee"

The origin of "Yankee" is a bit murky, but many scholars believe Mediterranean pirates coined the term as an epithet for Dutch seamen in the 1500s—and that it was probably derived from the common Dutch name Jan Kees, comparable to our John Doe. Later, Dutch settlers in New Amsterdam used it as a pejorative for hard-driving New England traders.

The term has had its ups and downs over 250 years. Yankee was not commonly used for Union soldiers in the Civil War, but Yank was popularized by the British as a fond nickname for their American Allies in World War I.

AN EARLY WIN FOR FREE SPEECH

The trial of newspaper publisher John Peter Zenger for "seditious libel" was a colonial sensation. Articles published in Zenger's *New-York Weekly Journal* often attacked the colony's governor, William Cosby, and his high-handed rule, until Cosby retaliated by throwing Zenger in jail.

The case came to trial eight months later, in 1735, and Zenger was represented by Scottish-born Andrew Hamilton, the first great "Philadelphia lawyer." Hamilton argued that truth is an absolute defense against libel and that the law, not his client, was at fault. The presiding judges were stooges for the governor, but the jury agreed with Hamilton and acquitted Zenger.

The Zenger victory is more important in hindsight than it was at the time. Most colonial judges and juries continued the English legal custom of disregarding truth in libel cases. Just seven years after ratifying the Bill of Rights with its guarantee of a free press, the U.S. Congress passed the Sedition Act of 1798 to shut down opposition to the Federalists. Not until a series of Supreme Court decisions in the 1960s and '70s did the American press win the clear right to publish—a freedom a colonial jury had awarded to Zenger.

THE FRENCH LOSE A WAR; WE WIN AN ALLY

The French and Indian War—part of nearly a century of conflict between France and Britain—went badly for the English at first, but the balance changed as British and colonial fighters mastered wilderness warfare. Under the 1763 Treaty of Paris, Britain gained control of France's North American territories east of the Mississippi River. For England, however, this victory also created serious problems, including how to pay off its huge war debt and handle its new American possessions.

For the colonies, these British difficulties led to more and higher taxes to help fill the British Treasury as well as increasingly restrictive British management. As American anger at Britain grew, alliances shifted, and France began to seem the better friend. So when the colonists rebelled in 1776, they looked to France as a natural ally. And with a little diplomatic persuasion, the French agreed—bringing Spanish support along for good measure.

After the Revolutionary War, however, relations with France became strained, primarily because the newly independent Americans increasingly favored the English. President John Adams narrowly avoided open warfare in 1800, restoring relations with our old ally.

Of Seals and Turkeys

America's first national emblem was the Great Seal of the United States, adopted by Congress in 1782. Selected by a series of committees from a number of designs, the seal aroused controversy. Benjamin Franklin supported the wild turkey as the emblem, not the American bald eagle, which he dismissed as "a bird of bad moral character."

The explanation of the pyramid on the reverse side of the seal comes from designer Charles Thomson, who wrote that the pyramid simply "signifies strength and duration," and the eye above it refers to "the many signal interpositions of providence in favor of the American cause." Other official symbols, emblems, songs, and patriotic declarations include:

Flag. The "Stars and Stripes" was adopted by the Continental Congress in 1777 and amended for the addition of stars representing new states. Flag Day, observed on June 14 since 1916, commemorates the day the Revolutionary Congress approved the design.

Anthem. "The Star-Spangled Banner" was written in 1814 by Francis Scott Key and set to the tune of the drinking song "Anacreon in Heaven." The song was recognized for official use in 1916 and adopted by Congress in 1931.

Motto. "In God we trust," possibly taken from the last stanza of "The Star-Spangled Banner," has been used on U.S. coins since 1864. It was adopted as the national motto in 1956.

Pledge. "The Pledge of Allegiance" was written by Francis Bellamy for *The Youth's Companion* magazine in 1892.

Creed. "The American's Creed" was written by William Tyler Page. The creed won a national competition and was adopted by Congress in 1918.

Christmas Tree. The General Grant Tree, a 1,600-plus-year-old giant sequoia in King's Canyon National Park in California, was proclaimed the nation's Christmas tree by President Coolidge in 1926 and made a national shrine in 1956.

Flower. The rose, variety unspecified, became our official national flower in 1983.

THE ROAD TO INDEPENDENCE

Bristling under British rule, the colonists found
leaders in the men we now call the Founding Fathers
and courage among countless farmers, tradespeople,
homemakers, slaves, and servants.

THE POCKETBOOK REBELLION

The colonists' first rebellion was economic. Colonists met a stream
of repressive English taxes and restrictions, including the Townshend Acts, by refusing to buy imported English goods. Ordinary
housewives were critical to the success of these protests because they
had to bear the brunt of giving up household staples from sugar and
spices to cloth and house paint. But the ladies and their families per-
severed, and the boycotts succeeded in getting a number of England's
onerous laws repealed.

The boycotts also had two other notable effects: They strength-
ened Britain's determination to get the independent-minded colonies
under control, and they forced many Americans to switch from a
soothing cuppa tea to a bitter brew of coffee—changing our national
taste in the process.

THANKS, BUT NO THANKS

The Tea Act of 1773 was intended to shore up an important London
business by creating a monopoly for the East India Company's tea
sales in the colonies. The Act actually brought the price of tea down
to bargain-basement level in an attempt to bankrupt American

merchants who couldn't compete—so the colonists had plenty of tea, but they were too furious at England's constant meddling to drink it.

Colonials at a number of American ports refused to unload the cheap tea from British ships. A band of Bostonians led by Samuel Adams went further and hosted a "tea party." Crudely dressed as American Indians—they made no effort to hide their true identities—the group dumped 350 crates of tea into Boston Harbor. English reprisals came in the form of the repressive "Intolerable Acts" of 1774, and set the stage for less polite conflict.

ENGLAND'S TOP 10 LEGAL BLUNDERS

Colonial Americans were riled by the gall of their English overlords. How dare they pass these restrictive laws—all intended to enrich the Royal Treasury and British business interests—without giving their colonists a voice in Parliament?

Navigation Acts of 1660 and 1673—limited colonial transport and trade in "enumerated commodities" (sugar, tobacco, cotton, indigo, dyewoods, and ginger) to England only

Wool Act of 1699—forbade export of some American-made textiles

Navigation Acts of 1704, 1705, and 1721—limited colonial trade in rice, naval stores (tar, pitch, turpentine, ship masts, and spars), copper, and furs

Hat Act of 1732—outlawed export of colonial-made hats

Molasses Act of 1733—imposed duties on imported molasses

Sugar Act of 1764—imposed duties on imported sugar, coffee, indigo, wine, pimento, and textiles

Stamp Act of 1765—levied taxes on all legal documents, newspapers, almanacs, playing cards, and dice

Quartering Act of 1765—required colonists to provide English military with living quarters, fire, candles, bedding, vinegar, salt, cider, beer, and rum

Townshend Revenue Act of 1767—levied duties on colonial imports of lead, paint, paper, glass, and tea

Tea Act of 1773—not a new tax, but an effort to boost East India Company sales by undercutting colonial merchants

THE MIDNIGHT RIDE OF WILLIAM DAWES?

Henry Wadsworth Longfellow's poem "Paul Revere's Ride" casts the colonial silversmith as a singular hero. But two riders—Revere and fellow Bostonian William Dawes—were dispatched to Lexington on that April night in 1775. Their mission: to warn Massachusetts colonists of British troop movements.

Revere took the shorter route, arriving in Lexington first. Deciding to ride to Concord, Revere and Dawes were joined along the way by Dr. Samuel Prescott (rumored to be returning from a romantic tryst). Stopped by a British patrol, Revere was escorted home at gunpoint, and Dawes escaped but became lost and was recaptured by the British. Prescott managed to reach Concord. In all, about 40 riders were roused from their beds to spread the alarm, enabling colonial Minutemen to assemble on Lexington Green, where the first shot of the Revolutionary War was fired the next day.

Dawes's descendants continued his tradition of service, including his great-great-grandson Charles Gates Dawes, U.S. vice president (1925–1929) and a recipient of the Nobel Peace Prize. Dr. Prescott joined the Continental Army and served as a battlefield surgeon, and died in British custody at age 26.

Eat, Drink, and Plot a Revolution

Rebellious colonists did more than down tankards of ale at their local taverns. These gathering spots—three of which still exist today—provided safety for leaders of the colonial rebellion as they planned and plotted against the English. Five taverns that played significant roles are:

Green Dragon Tavern, Boston—Paul Revere called it "the cradle of liberty." Located in Boston's North End, the Green Dragon was the site of regular meetings of the Sons of Liberty, the Boston Committee of Correspondence, and other rebellious groups. The Boston Tea Party was plotted here in 1773, and eyewitnesses reported seeing Samuel Adams's "Indians" sneaking out the back door on their way to Boston Harbor.

Raleigh Tavern, Williamsburg, Virginia—Defiant legislators met here whenever the royal governor dissolved the colony's House of Burgesses, which often happened. In 1774 Patrick Henry, Thomas Jefferson, Francis Lighthorse Lee, and others devised the Committees of Correspondence (an intercolonial communication system for secretly exchanging information) in the tavern's Apollo Room. The Marquis de Lafayette, a hero of the Revolutionary War, was feted here during his 1824 visit to America.

Fraunces Tavern, New York City—In 1765 a British sea captain whose ship carried English tea was brought to the Fraunces and forced to publicly apologize for his country's oppressive taxes. Afterward, New Yorkers staged the first "tea party," tossing the captain's cargo into New York Harbor. The tavern survived a British cannonball in the war, and in 1783 General George Washington bade farewell to his officers here before resigning his commission as their commander.

Indian Queen Tavern, Philadelphia—A popular meeting place for members of the Continental Congress, the Indian Queen gave shelter to Thomas Jefferson while he was drafting the Declaration of Independence in the summer of 1776. It had also hosted Ben Franklin and his Junto Club of colonial intellectuals.

Tun Tavern, Philadelphia—An early brew house, the Tun served many Revolutionary War leaders and politicians excellent beer and "Red Hot Beef Steak" prepared by Peggy Mullan, the wife of the tavern owner. On November 10, 1775, when the Continental Congress authorized the formation of a Marine Corps, Robert Mullan was appointed chief marine recruiter. Mullan's tavern served as the first recruiting station, and to this day, U.S. Marines celebrate Tun Tavern on November 10.

PERFECTING AMERICA'S FIRST DOCUMENT

The final draft of the Declaration of Independence had included a number of revisions by the five-member committee appointed by the Continental Congress to write it, and not all the changes were to the liking of its temperamental author, Thomas Jefferson. After writing an initial draft, Jefferson gave it to Benjamin Franklin and John Adams for their comments. Adams later said he didn't remember any criticisms, and Jefferson recalled, "Their alterations were two or three only, and merely verbal." But handwritten notes, edits, and strikethroughs on the early draft copy show that Franklin and Adams had more than a little to contribute. Congress also made a number of alterations and additions and deleted two paragraphs before adopting the Declaration by unanimous vote.

As historians have pointed out, Jefferson's opening passages may be a glorious statement of enlightened principles, but what really mattered to the Founding Fathers was their lengthy list of grievances against the British crown, stated boldly and with merit.

MISTRESS OF THE PRINTING PRESS

There's no question that the Founders had a lot of faith in Mary Katherine Goddard, a Baltimore printer. As soon as the ink was dry, they entrusted the first signed copy of the Declaration of Independence to her. (The first printing of the document, known as the "Dunlap Broadsides," didn't include the signers' names.)

Born in Connecticut, Mary Katherine and her brother, William, owned print shops and published newspapers in Providence and Philadelphia before moving to Baltimore, where William started and Mary Katherine published the city's first newspaper. By all accounts a skilled printer and manager respected by her male employees, Mary Katherine was also known as a fair and impartial editor—unusual at a time when everyone else was so full of opinions.

A REVOLUTION LIKE NO OTHER

ALTHOUGH MANY COLONISTS HAD NO DESIRE TO SEPARATE FROM ENGLAND, THE FORCES OF FREEDOM PREVAILED, AND THE NEWLY DECLARED AND ILL-PREPARED UNITED STATES OF AMERICA WENT TO WAR.

THE MAKING OF A COMMANDER

As a member of the Virginia militia, the young George Washington served in the French and Indian War and was discharged with the honorary title of brigadier general, in spite of his brave but less than stellar performance in battle. He then married and retired to Mount Vernon, proving himself a gifted agronomist.

Almost two decades later, his yen for honor and glory resurfaced at the Second Continental Congress. As a delegate, Washington spoke little but wore his old blue-and-buff militia uniform every day as a signal that he wanted to lead the new Continental Army. His fellow delegates agreed and, at age 47, the general took command.

UNCLE SAM'S OLDER BROTHER

Before Uncle Sam, Americans had Brother Jonathan, a fictional patriot possibly based on Governor Jonathan Trumbull of Connecticut, a fervent supporter of the American Revolution and friend of George Washington. Brother Jonathan—the antithesis of John Bull, Britain's mythical mascot—was pictured in political cartoons looking a lot like Uncle Sam, but younger, jollier, and beardless.

DIDN'T HAPPEN!

Betsy Ross's Flagging Reputation

Mrs. Ross probably didn't make the first American flag, although she may have had some influence on its design. Her legend comes from a family story first made public in 1870, and even the family member who told the tale warned that it might not be accurate.

A better claimant to the stars-and-stripes design is Francis Hopkinson, a signer of the Declaration of Independence and a member of the committee that selected the nation's Great Seal. At least Hopkinson had submitted an itemized bill to Congress for his work on the flag and received partial payment.

BLACK SOLDIERS ON THE FRONT LINES

In October 1775 General Washington, a slave owner, barred all recruitment of blacks for service in the Continental Army even though black patriots had fought at Lexington and Concord. A month later, Lord Dunmore, the royal governor of Virginia, offered freedom to slaves and indentured whites who would fight on the British side and Washington was soon forced to reverse his decision. In time more than 5,000 black soldiers and sailors, both slaves and free men, fought in the Continental Army and Navy—most in integrated units.

After the Battle of Yorktown, approximately 20,000 slaves who fought on the British side were left in limbo, and Sir Guy Carleton, acting commander of the British forces after General Cornwallis's defeat, adamantly refused to allow black loyalists to be handed back into slavery. An estimated 3,000 to 4,000 former slaves who had served with the Brits fled to New York City, where they were registered and then transported for resettlement as free people in Canada, the British West Indies, and England. Others managed to escape the country by various routes. Many more, including some black patriots, were returned as "property" to their American owners.

WOMEN AT THE RAMPARTS

Margaret Corbin was at her husband's side and took over the cannons when he was killed during the Battle of Fort Washington in 1776, loading and firing until she was seriously injured. Her wounds left her badly scarred, and she permanently lost the use of her left arm. She was awarded a disabled soldier's pension for her bravery. Buried without ceremony, she is now interred in the war cemetery at the U.S. Military Academy at West Point.

Mrs. Corbin was just one of the never-say-die women who fought on the battlefields. Known collectively by the nickname "Molly Pitcher," they were often soldiers' wives, widows, or sisters who enlisted to serve with the army and state militias or help in field hospitals. Although every army has its "camp followers" (the time-honored euphemism for prostitutes), scholars believe their numbers were relatively low for the Continental Army, mainly because camp conditions were so poor and food so scarce.

"The Secret Soldier"

Deborah Sampson's ancestors arrived on the *Mayflower* but her family hit hard times, and she spent most of her childhood as an indentured servant. At 21, eager to participate in the Revolutionary War, Deborah disguised herself as a man and enlisted in the Massachusetts militia as an infantry soldier, fighting as "Robert Shurtleff" (her deceased brother) for almost two years.

When rumors of her deception spread in her hometown, she was excommunicated in absentia by her Baptist church for "dressing in men's clothing." Badly wounded at Tarrytown, she treated herself. Later, when she contracted a fever in Philadelphia, an Army doctor discovered her secret, and General Washington himself may have been told. Neither man betrayed her, and under her assumed name, she received an honorable discharge as "Robert Shurtleff." Her subsequent efforts to receive a military pension were championed by Paul Revere.

A SHREWD PUBLIC RELATIONS GENIUS

While representing the Continental Congress, Benjamin Franklin traveled to Paris to help negotiate an alliance with France against England. Dressed in his humble Quaker clothes and rustic fur hat, Franklin was greeted enthusiastically by the French as the living symbol of American independence. He charmed the elites with his eccentric style and intellectual conversation while he was cunningly convincing the French foreign minister, the Comte de Vergennes, to sign two treaties and openly enter the war on the American side.

A SOLDIER'S NECESSITIES

At the start of the Revolution, the average colonial infantryman probably didn't have a uniform, but he had (or was supplied with) the following necessities:

Flintlock musket with bayonet. In close-order battle, the quick-loading flintlock was preferred over the more accurate but slower to reload American rifle. American rifles (aka "Pennsylvania" or "Kentucky"), with three times the range of muskets, were favored by soldiers on guard or in flanking positions.

Bayonet or spontoon (a long metal spearhead mounted on a wooden pike).

Sword. Infantry officers used hunting or small swords. Cavalry carried heavy sabers.

Tomahawk or ax. Essential when a man didn't have a bayonet or spear.

Cartridge bag containing cartridge paper, lead balls, and black powder. Riflemen carried powder horns and shot bags.

Flint and tinderbox for starting fires

Hunting knife

Knapsack and blanket

**Canteen, folding eating utensils, scissors, fishhook
and sinker**

Sundial compass

WHEN PAYMENT WAS DUE

Revolutionary leaders quickly realized that the wheels of war don't turn on high principles. Money was in short supply in 1776, but two men—Haym Salomon, a Polish-Jewish immigrant to New York, and Robert Morris, superintendent for finance for the colonies—worked closely and found the cash, often from their own coffers.

When the British took New York, Salomon lost his brokerage business and was almost hanged as a traitor, but he escaped to Philadelphia and rebuilt his business there. A close confidant of General Washington and other founders, Salomon continued to raise and administer funds, including subsidies from France and Holland, for the Continental Army. He also supported other patriots including Thomas Jefferson and James Madison with personal loans, for which he never asked to be repaid.

VIVE LE COMTE!

A large contingent of French naval and ground forces, under the command of Comte Donatien Rochambeau, landed at Newport, Rhode Island, in 1780, and they were all set to fight for the Americans. But the Americans had gone, and so had most of the British. The people of Newport, however, welcomed the French troops in their elegant uniforms, so Rochambeau decided to wait until he could meet with General Washington.

It was a good thing, too. Not only did the two leaders plot out the successful Southern strategy that would end the war, but the

Comte also provided desperately needed funds for the Continental Army—$20,000 in gold, which was half of the French commander's war chest.

KING'S MOUNTAIN: THE ALL-AMERICAN BATTLE

Many Americans loyal to England fought for the British in the Southern colonies, but only one battle was waged entirely by colonists on both sides. The sole Brit on hand was Major Patrick Ferguson, who commanded the loyalist militia.

Their patriot opponents were an irregular army of tough Appalachian pioneers. When Ferguson threatened to "hang their leaders and lay their country waste with fire and sword," he enraged these "over-mountain men" known for their aversion to authority and their sheer cussedness.

The clash came on October 7, 1780, at King's Mountain, a pine-forested hill on the border between South and North Carolina. Ferguson and his troops held the hilltop, assuming they could easily pick off all enemies coming from below. But the mountain men had backwoods cunning and long-range rifles. Dodging from tree to tree, they scaled the slope and overwhelmed the loyalists in 65 minutes.

The loyalists suffered more than 400 dead or wounded, including Ferguson; 29 frontiersmen died. History credits this victory with precipitating General Cornwallis's retreat to Charleston, leading to his defeat at Yorktown a year later.

OLD SOLDIERS' CLUB SHOCKER

Many Americans were shocked by the formation of the General Society of the Cincinnati in 1783. Named for Lucius Quintus Cincinnatus, an ancient Roman farmer and conquering general, the group limited membership to former officers in the Continental Army and Navy.

Membership was to be passed from father to eldest son, reminding critics of the British nobility's inheritance custom of primogeniture.

America's own Cincinnatus, George Washington, served as first president, although he didn't approve of the inherited membership. However benign, the old soldiers' club struck others as too close to English elitism and a threat to the principle that "all men are created equal"—prompting a rare backlash in the public's high opinion of Washington.

IF AT FIRST YOU DON'T SUCCEED . . .

After the Revolution, Americans were left asking, What next? Their first effort at self-government, the Articles of Confederation, basically gave control to the new states under the eye of an impotent and insolvent federal Congress. The states quickly proved incapable of playing nicely with one another or resolving their arguments to anyone's satisfaction. The outcome of this experiment was failure, but in the process, the country and its leaders learned what worked and what didn't—knowledge they used to craft the Constitution.

HAS ANYONE SEEN RHODE ISLAND?

Forming a strong government to replace the Confederation was necessary but not universally popular. The small states knew they were outnumbered in population and power, and Rhode Island, which was also contending with heavy debts, protested by sending zero delegates to the Constitutional Convention in Philadelphia. In fact, only 55 of the 74 state delegates invited to the convention showed up—some arriving months behind schedule—and a measly 39 men signed the Constitution they finally hammered out.

Opponents including Patrick Henry and George Mason kept the pot boiling during the ratification process. The outcome was seriously

October 17: A Double Whammy

Strictly by coincidence, two of the most important battles of the Revolutionary War occurred on October 17. The Revolutionaries bested the Redcoats at the Battle of Saratoga (New York) on October 17, 1777—a major turning point in the war. Over the next four years, the war moved southward into Virginia, where General Cornwallis and his 7,200 English troopers were forced to surrender on October 17, 1781 at Yorktown, ending the colonists' five-year-long war for independence.

in doubt until the 1788 publication of *The Federalist,* a collection of 85 carefully reasoned, pro-Constitution essays written under the pseudonym Publius by James Madison, Alexander Hamilton, and John Jay. Printed serially in newspapers and then as a book, *The Federalist* turned the tide. New York and Virginia, the holdout states that held the key to ratification, fell into line. It was a close call. But even Rhode Island, the stubborn straggler, finally showed up.

INAUGURATED, NOT CROWNED

Many true patriots argued for a monarchy, but wiser heads prevailed and the United States of America became the first nation in history to have an elected president. To no one's surprise, the man chosen was George Washington, who initially declined the offer.

Washington was sworn in on April 30, 1789 on a balcony of Federal Hall in New York City—his brief speech barely audible to the crowd below. Then he delivered the country's first formal presidential address to members of Congress and fellow patriots inside the hall. Accounts by those present say the president trembled as he spoke, not from age or nerves, but from his deep understanding of the challenges ahead.

Start-Up to Superpower

Our Government and Growth

After independence, Americans had to construct a nation. The abundance of land and natural resources attracted an increasingly diverse immigrant population. Western expansion was unstoppable, and each new territory ratcheted up the conflict over slavery and the march to war. With the Union restored, industry boomed, but the gulf between the very rich and average Americans widened. In the 20th century, the United States fought two world wars and established itself as a military and economic power to be reckoned with.

A ROCKY START

THE NEW UNITED STATES HAD ITS CONSTITUTION, PRESIDENT, CONGRESS, AND LITTLE ELSE. NOTHING LIKE THIS SELF-GOVERNING REPUBLIC HAD EVER BEEN TRIED BEFORE, AND THE NATION STRUGGLED TO DEFINE ITSELF.

GEORGE WASHINGTON SETS THE TONE

John Adams, a lover of pomp and protocol, wanted to address the new president as "His Elective Majesty." Someone else suggested "His High Mightiness." Washington opted for the simple "Mr. President." Titles and forms of address, ceremonies and events, White House etiquette, voluntary limits on terms: All bore the distinctive touch of the man from Mount Vernon.

Most important, he defined the nature of the presidency by selecting people of proven ability to serve in key positions and giving them the authority to do their jobs, seeking out wise counsel, and guiding rather than dictating policy.

THE MACHINE THAT MADE COTTON KING

By the end of the 18th century, there were signs that the cotton-based economy of the South was faltering, raising hopes in some quarters that the institution of slavery would soon become too expensive and die out. Then Eli Whitney invented the cotton gin. By mechanizing the removal of seeds from picked cotton—an exceptionally time- and labor-intensive process when done by hand—Whitney's invention resuscitated the cotton industry and inadvertently prolonged slavery for another half century.

TRYING TO END THE SLAVE TRADE?

Before there was a United States, the Continental Congress temporarily prohibited importation of slaves to damage England's economy. In a compromise with Southern delegates, the Constitutional Convention mandated abolition of the slave trade by 1808, though the legality of owning slaves was never addressed. (The American system of slavery was self-perpetuating because slaves *and their descendents* were held in bondage for life, unless freed by their owners.)

Unfortunately, the 1808 law ending the trade in humans was largely ignored, and illegal trafficking in imported slaves—an estimated half million Africans—continued until the Civil War.

MAD MONEY

Maybe the most important question facing our new nation was how to pay for itself, and Alexander Hamilton, the first Treasury Secretary, was the man with the plan. Basically, Hamilton proposed paying off all federal and state debts at face value and then creating a national bank funded by the government and private investors. Hamilton's first proposal prompted many Congressmen to buy up nearly worth-

Playing Down-and-Dirty

The presidential campaign of 1800 pitted incumbent John Adams against his vice president, Thomas Jefferson. Ideological differences between the two Founding Fathers became vicious mudslinging in the hands of supporters, especially after Jefferson paid journalist/polemicist James Thomson Callender to be his chief attack dog. The volatile, heavy-drinking Callender did the job too well and was convicted and imprisoned for sedition.

Jefferson won the election but angered Callender by not being sufficiently generous with presidential favors. In retaliation, Callender revealed Jefferson's intimate relationship with Sally Hemmings, his slave, in a series of articles published in 1802.

less government IOUs, called "certificates," from the Revolutionary War and Confederation years, a disgraceful scramble to profit from the losses of their fellow citizens.

Congressman James Madison offered a fairer alternative, which quickly failed, and argued forcefully against the Bank of the United States, but Hamilton got what he wanted. Though the national bank didn't survive the partisan politics of the early 1800s, the broad outline of his plan to promote industrial growth and trade by favoring local and foreign investment remains to this day.

THE SUPREMES FIND THEIR VOICE

The importance of *Marbury v. Madison,* decided in 1803 by the Supreme Court under John Marshall, the second Chief Justice, wasn't what happened to the litigants but the emergence of the core principle of the Court's authority to rule on the constitutionality of congressional and, by implication, presidential actions. Marshall's written opinion was legal genius and began the Court's transformation from a glorified night court into a robust third branch of government.

THE NATION DOUBLES IN SIZE

The Louisiana Purchase was perhaps the slickest real estate deal in our history—more than 2 million square acres, including the essential port of New Orleans and the mouth of the Mississippi River, was bought for less than 3 cents an acre. Negotiations with France were tricky, and there were questions about whether the Constitution gave President Jefferson the power to make such a deal. But in the end, Napoleon needed the money. The final cost, with interest, was a mere $27,300,000.

THE PIRATE WAR THAT STILL RANKLES

The pirate nations of North Africa's Barbary Coast long controlled the Mediterranean Sea, raiding foreign commercial ships and demanding tribute. But when the United States refused to pay off the pasha of Tripoli in 1801, the pasha declared war. President Jefferson assembled a ragtag navy of warships that brought the pirates to heel in 1804.

How We've Grown

The United States expanded by acquiring land, sometimes through negotiation and sometimes by force.

1803 The Louisiana Purchase, bought from France

1819 Florida, ceded by Spain (Adams-Onis Treaty)

1842 Northern Maine, ceded by Britain (Webster-Ashburton Treaty)

1845 Texas, annexed and admitted to statehood

1846 Oregon Territory, divided between the United States and Britain at the 49th parallel (Buchanan-Parkenham Treaty)

1848 Southwest Territories, comprising California, New Mexico, and the Rio Grande River border, ceded in the Treaty of Guadalupe Hidalgo ended the Mexican-American War

1893 Gadsden Purchase, bought from Spain

1867 Alaska, purchased from Russia

1898 Puerto Rico, Guam, and the Philippines, ceded by treaty after the Spanish-American War (The Phillippines became independent in 1935.)

1898 Hawaii, annexed following coup engineered by American business interests

1899 American Samoa, annexed

1917 U.S. Virgin Islands, purchased from Denmark

Earlier efforts to deal peacefully with the pirate state included a "Treaty of peace and friendship" with Tripoli that remains controversial. Article 11 begins, "As the government of the United States of America is not in any sense founded on the Christian religion...." Ratified by Congress in June 1797, this treaty was superseded 8 years later and would have been forgotten long ago but for Article 11. No one knows why the religion clause was included; it doesn't appear in similar treaties with Algeria and Tunis. The wording wasn't questioned in 1797, it survives as a sore spot in church/state debates.

AN EXPLORER'S MYSTERIOUS DEMISE

Sent to the Pacific Northwest on a mission of exploration by President Jefferson, Meriwether Lewis and William Clark became the heroes of the nation. After their return in 1806, Jefferson appointed Lewis governor of the Louisiana Territory.

In 1809, on a journey to Washington, Lewis stopped at an inn in western Tennessee. The next morning, he was found shot several times, and died soon after. His death was ruled a suicide, but many believed it was murder. Modern scholarship indicates it may have been accidental.

RESTOCKING THE LIBRARY OF CONGRESS

One reason Thomas Jefferson was so often in need of money was his addiction to books, which he purchased by the crateload. As president, he took a personal hand in selecting titles for the new Library of Congress in Washington. In 1814, after learning that the British had destroyed the collection during their rampage in the capital, Jefferson offered his own library, at a price. It was a good bargain for both sides: The former president got much-needed cash and the Library of Congress was rebuilt on the best private collection—about 6,000 volumes—in the nation.

DIDN'T HAPPEN!

Dolley's Last-Minute Save

American schoolchildren heard the story for more than a century—how on April 24, 1814, Dolley Madison, with invading British soldiers at the door, dashed back into the White House to personally snatch Gilbert Stuart's full-length portrait of George Washington from the wall. The day before, she had written to her sister about her determination to save the famous portrait.

While there's no question about the First Lady's courage under fire, recent historical research indicates that her letter was probably written many years after the White House was burned and that Mrs. Madison may have ordered the portrait saved, but others accomplished the rescue.

ALL ROADS LEAD WEST

If the country was to grow and prosper, it needed roadways to link established cities and open the way to the West. Our first road-building boom, from around 1810 to 1850, was the start of the highway system we have today.

The National Road (now U.S. Route 40) ran from Cumberland, Maryland to Vandalia, Illinois, closely following the military trail opened by General Edward Braddock and a young militia officer named George Washington during the French and Indian War. Congress authorized funding for the National Road in 1806, making it the first federally financed highway in our history.

ADAMS AND JEFFERSON: FRIENDS AT THE END

John Adams and Thomas Jefferson were often at odds during the early days of the republic. But with age came respect and a goodly measure of reconciliation, if not agreement.

The men corresponded until their deaths, within hours of one another, on July 4, 1826—the 50th anniversary of the Declaration of

Independence, which they had, of course, fought about. Jefferson died first, and Adams, who didn't know of his friend's passing, is reported to have said "Jefferson" just before he expired several hours later.

Saving a Friend from the Blade

As the First Lady with the misfortune to follow the universally popular Dolley Madison, Elizabeth Kortright Monroe, a beautiful and cultured New Yorker, was regarded by many as cold and aloof. Critics complained that her years in Paris, as the wife of the American ambassador, turned her head. But coolness had served Elizabeth well when she challenged French authority in 1795, at the height of the Reign of Terror. Learning that Adrienne de Lafayette, the wife of the Marquis de Lafayette—Revolutionary War hero and President Washington's great friend— was imprisoned and probably destined for the guillotine, Mrs. Monroe summoned the American Embassy's carriage and went, by herself and very publicly, to the prison to visit Adrienne.

Taken as an unofficial signal of American concern, Elizabeth's daring act prompted French officials to release Adrienne rather than damage relations with the United States. In France, Elizabeth became known affectionately as "la belle Americaine," as much for her diplomatic skills as her looks.

ELECTORAL COLLEGE TWISTS AND TURNS

Our Electoral College is always confusing and often frustrating. Not until the passage of the Twelfth Amendment did citizens get the opportunity to vote for electors. Even so, four U.S. presidents were not the people's choice. The 2000 contest between Vice President Al Gore and Governor George W. Bush is just the most recent example.

- In 1824 Andrew Jackson won the plurality of the people's votes (41.3 percent), but not the required Electoral College majority. The decision went to the House of Representatives, which chose John Quincy Adams. In their 1828 rematch, Jackson easily defeated Adams.

- In 1876 Rutherford B. Hayes faced Samuel J. Tilden. When Tilden won 51 percent of the popular vote, the Electoral College, riddled with factional and regional conflicts, couldn't come to a decision. So the House of Representatives crafted a compromise and elected Hayes.

- In 1888 Benjamin Harrison challenged President Grover Cleveland in what is regarded as the most corrupt presidential election in U.S. history. Although Cleveland led by a nose in the popular vote, Harrison won the Electoral College.

JACKSON'S INAUGURAL MADHOUSE

Previous inaugurations were stately affairs, so no one expected 20,000 Americans to gather below the Capitol steps and watch Andrew Jackson take the oath of office in March 1829. Francis Scott Key proclaimed the sight "beautiful . . . sublime!"

Rejecting a traditional post-inaugural celebration, "Old Hickory" opened the White House to all comers. Thousands trooped through that afternoon and evening, enjoying free food and wine punch and jostling to shake the President's hand. Lacking any policing or crowd control, the reception turned raucous. People climbed through windows and onto the furniture. China and glasses were smashed, and costly upholstery and carpets were damaged beyond repair. Fearing

Young Hickory as POW

During the Revolutionary War, 13-year-old Andy Jackson and his brother Robert joined a local Carolina regiment as couriers. Nabbed by the British and nearly starved in captivity, both boys contracted smallpox, and Robert died a few days after their mother secured their release. All of Jackson's immediate family, including his beloved mother and eldest brother, perished during the war, leaving the future President with a lifelong distaste for the British.

for Jackson's safety, aides hustled him away. Supreme Court Justice Joseph Story declared, "The reign of KING MOB seemed triumphant." Outgoing President John Quincy Adams missed the chaos by sullenly refusing to attend the inauguration.

WHAT KIND OF DESTINY?

The concept of "Manifest Destiny" first appeared in an 1839 article by John O'Sullivan, editor of the magazine *Democratic Review,* and O'Sullivan used the term explicitly in a later piece urging annexation of Texas.

Originally little more than a political slogan, this grandiose theory that U.S. expansion across the continent was divinely and obviously ordained fit neatly into the wave of religious fervor then sweeping the United States. "Manifest Destiny" soon became embedded in the national psyche as the expression of what many saw as the country's mission to establish Protestant Anglo-Saxon hegemony from sea to shining sea.

A TRAGEDY THAT BEGAN WITH GOLD

It started with the 1828 discovery of gold on Cherokee tribal land in Georgia, leading to conflict between private speculators and the Indians. After the Supreme Court ruled that Georgia couldn't impose state laws within Cherokee territory, the Jackson Administration attempted to open up the valuable land through voluntary relocation of the Cherokee. In 1838 President Martin Van Buren finally ordered a forced removal.

Approximately 16,000 Cherokees and 2,000 black slaves were rounded up at gunpoint, held in filthy camps, and then set out on the long march to the Oklahoma territory. Deaths on the "Trail of Tears" are estimated at between 2,000 and 6,000, most from disease and the rigors of the 1,200-mile trek.

GOOD GUY FINISHES LAST

Nicholas P. Trist, friend and confidant of presidents and famous men, was beside Thomas Jefferson when the Founding Father died. He became Andrew Jackson's personal secretary and worked for James Buchanan at the State Department. A lawyer with extensive foreign service credentials, fluent in Spanish, and a loyal Democrat with no political ambitions, Trist seemed the perfect choice to negotiate peace with the Mexicans when President James K. Polk dispatched him on a secret mission to Veracruz in 1847.

Freedom Writer

As an apprentice journalist in Boston, William Lloyd Garrison acquired writing and editing skills while shaping his commitment to the immediate abolition of slavery. In 1831, at age 26, he published the first edition of *The Liberator,* voicing his take-no-prisoners determination to see that "every chain be broken and every bondman set free!"

In print and in person, his radicalism was so intense that the state of Georgia put up a $5,000 bounty for his arrest, and he was once nearly lynched by an anti-abolition Boston mob. Though he advocated nonviolent resistance, his rhetoric alienated some close allies, including Frederick Douglass. Garrison continued publishing *The Liberator* until the Civil War ended, then turned his talents to other reforms. When he died in 1879, flags were flown at half-staff throughout Boston, and Douglass spoke warmly of the man "who could stand alone with the truth."

But things didn't go smoothly. Polk—anxious to end his unpopular Mexican War and frustrated by Trist's apparent lack of progress—ordered him recalled. By the time Trist received that news, however, he was close to a settlement and chose to ignore Polk's instructions. The resulting Treaty of Guadalupe Hidalgo achieved everything Polk wanted, but the president was furious with his disobedient diplomat. Returning to Washington, Trist was immediately fired and denied his salary, and his reputation was ruined. Despite the efforts of friends, the best jobs Trist could find were low-level positions, and the negotiator who concluded one of the best peace deals in American history died a forgotten man.

MAKE THAT *GALLANT* OLD PARTY

The Republican Party, formed in 1854 by opponents of the Kansas-Nebraska Act, included many refugees from the two dominant political parties, the Whigs and the Democrats. Though considered a minority party, Republicans put Abraham Lincoln in the presidency just six years after their formation. GOP, traced back to 1875, apparently stood for "Gallant Old Party"—not "Grand Old Party," as most people suppose.

AN EARLY PLOT ON LINCOLN'S LIFE?

Abraham Lincoln's whistle-stop journey to Washington for his 1861 inauguration would take him through Baltimore, where, warned Allen Pinkerton, an assassination attempt was planned. Founder of the Pinkerton National Detective Agency, the former Chicago cop had been hired by the railroad to protect the president-elect.

Under tight security, Lincoln was transported through Baltimore in the dead of night—his private railcar pulled by horses to avoid any sound—and arrived safely in Washington around dawn. When his scheduled train stopped in Baltimore the next morning, the waiting crowd turned angry on learning that the president-elect was not aboard.

Whether the plot was real is still debated. But Lincoln was immediately subjected to ridicule in the press, and stories of his "cowardice" dogged him until his death—by an assassin's bullet.

DIDN'T HAPPEN!

The Dashed-Off Gettysburg Address

Lincoln didn't write the Gettysburg Address on the back of an envelope on his way to the November 19, 1863, dedication of the Pennsylvania cemetery. He wrote and rewrote his moving Gettysburg speech well in advance and also edited the written version distributed to the press to include the words "under God," which he had added while speaking.

Lincoln kept his remarks short because he wasn't the main speaker of the day. That honor went to former Harvard president Edward Everett, whose two-hour oration has not been long remembered.

DRAFT SCAMS, CIVIL WAR–STYLE

Both sides drafted soldiers during the Civil War. Southern conscription, instituted in 1862, was efficiently straightforward. With very few exceptions, able-bodied men aged 18 to 35 could be called up at any time by the Confederate president.

The Union's 1863 draft plan, however, was a bureaucratic nightmare of quotas for states and congressional districts combined with federal, state, and local bounties (cash payments to men who signed up on their own). Bounties were supposed to encourage voluntary service. Instead, they created legions of "bounty jumpers" who deserted after getting their payments and repeatedly re-enlisted, collecting more bounties under different names.

Even worse were exemptions for men wealthy enough to either pay a "commutation fee" of $300 or hire substitute soldiers to take their place in combat. These escape valves for the privileged few sparked widespread protests and actually hurt recruitment.

THE BLOODIEST DAY

The Battle of Antietam, or Sharpsville, should have been a triumph for the Confederacy. Under General Robert E. Lee's command, the Johnny Rebs were pushing north, defeating Union forces at the Second Battle of Bull Run (August 29 to 30, 1862) and forcing their retreat. The decisive battle came on September 17 at Antietam Creek in Maryland. Southern forces were badly outnumbered—about 55,000 soldiers to Union General George McClellan's 87,000—but highly motivated.

The battle raged from daybreak till after dark. In the end, the outcome was a draw, but Lee's northward advance had been halted. In human terms, both sides took terrible losses. In all, an estimated 7,000 men died of their wounds in battle or later, and all casualties exceeded 27,000—the largest one-day total in America's military history.

CONFUSED ON THE BORDER

When the Confederate states seceded, four slave states—Kentucky, Missouri, Maryland, and Delaware—stayed in the Union. To hold the loyalty of these "border states," President Lincoln delayed issuing the Emancipation Proclamation until January 1, 1863. By then, the tide of battle was shifting to the North, diminishing the influence of Confederate sympathizers in the original border states and the newly admitted state of West Virginia. Lincoln's proclamation applied only to Confederate states and areas actively engaged "in rebellion"—not the border states.

Oddly, one Confederate state, Tennessee, wasn't mentioned in Lincoln's executive order, but the omission was no accident. About a third of the state's population was strongly pro-Union, and Tennessee—home of Lincoln's vice president, Andrew Johnson—had been reluctant to join the Confederacy. The last state to secede, it became the first state of the Old Confederacy readmitted to the Union.

"CRAZY BET": CIVIL WAR SPY

Elizabeth Van Lew, daughter of a wealthy Virginia family, became an ardent abolitionist while attending school in Philadelphia. Her fanatic support of the Union earned the contempt of her neighbors in Richmond, the Confederate capital, but most people decided the sharp-tongued spinster with the piercing blue eyes was simply not right in the head.

No one imagined that "Crazy Bet," the town pariah—a persona she played to the hilt—might be a spy. Among her many exploits was placing Mary Elizabeth Bower, a freed slave and Lizzie's confidant, inside Jefferson Davis's household to gather intelligence. When Richmond fell to General Grant, one of the first people he and his wife visited was Miss Van Lew—a signal that "Crazy Bet" had his special protection.

GRANT'S COMPASSIONATE CHOICE

Early on the morning of April 9, 1865, a Confederate rider bore a white flag onto a Virginia battlefield. Surprised Union troopers were told that General Robert E. Lee requested a meeting with General Ulysses Grant. Lee arrived first in the tiny town of Appomattox Court House. He knew the Southern cause was lost and was prepared to surrender his army. But what would Grant want? Revenge or reconciliation?

Thanks to the wisdom of two like-minded generals, the terms were simple, humane, and honorable. Grant pledged that if Lee's men laid down their weapons and went home, there would be no reprisals. Knowing that most of the Rebel soldiers would be returning to long-neglected farms, Grant let them keep their horses and mules. As news of Lee's surrender spread among the Union troops, they started firing artillery in celebration, until Grant ordered the cannons silenced. Peace had begun.

DIDN'T HAPPEN!

The Legend of Barbara Frietchie

Poet John Greenleaf Whittier penned "Barbara Frietchie" in 1863 to honor an elderly Union loyalist who boldly waved the Stars and Stripes from her attic window in the face of General Stonewall Jackson and his brigade as they trooped past her house in Frederick, Maryland. But Whittier's much-loved verses ("'Shoot, if you must, this old gray head/But spare your country's flag,' she said.") were pure myth.

Mrs. Frietchie (or Fritchie) was 95 years old and, according to her nephew and executor, confined to bed. The Confederates' route didn't pass her house that day, and Jackson had left Frederick before his men arrived. Whittier defended his sources for the story, though Mrs. Frietchie, who died in 1862, wasn't around to confirm or deny.

"JIM CROW" LAYS DOWN THE LAWS

During Reconstruction, federal troops were sent South to protect black and white citizens alike from the murderous brutalities of the Ku Klux Klan and other rabid segregationists. Then in 1876 the rest of the country, weary of Southern problems, voted for Rutherford B. Hayes and his promise to end Reconstruction. President Hayes pulled the military out, and as an immediate consequence, Southern legislators flooded their states with hundreds of laws depriving blacks of their recently acquired legal rights.

These laws—nicknamed "Jim Crow" for a black-face character popularized by white minstrel show performers—were upheld and enforced, often with stunning cruelty, well into the 20th century.

THE GREAT RAILROAD ROBBERY

The 1869 completion of America's transcontinental railroad was hailed as a triumph of progress. Three years later, the public learned

"Exodusters" Head to Kansas

In a spontaneous reaction to the collapse of Reconstruction, thousands of poor blacks in the Deep South packed their few belongings in the spring of 1879 and traveled up the Mississippi River. The goal was Kansas, the "promised land" to many former slaves. By the boatload they stopped first in St. Louis, then continued upriver to Kansas towns—Wyandotte, Leavenworth, Atchison.

Taken by surprise, local and state officials and citizens scrambled to provide food and shelter and organize some way to resettle the "Exodusters." For the most part, Kansans proved generous and resourceful, and with great difficulty, they accommodated the newcomers. This unplanned year-long exodus from the South increased Kansas's population by an estimated 6,000 to 10,000.

that it had also spawned the worst case of graft and corruption the nation had yet experienced. The complicated scam involved a dummy construction company, the Credit Mobilier, used to divert government funds into the pockets of Thomas Durant and Oliver Ames, both officers of the Union Pacific Railroad, and their cronies. The railroad men were abetted by Ames's brother, Oakes, a powerful member of the House of Representatives, and more than a dozen other Congressmen.

The scandal broke when Durant sued Oliver Ames for control of the Union Pacific and the names of Credit Mobilier shareholders became public. Politicians were embarrassed, but no one was ever charged with a crime, and there was never a full accounting of the tens of millions of public dollars lost to greed.

PIUTE TRUTH-TELLER

American Indian history and culture were not familiar to most Americans when Sarah Winnemucca's autobiography, *Life Among the Piutes: Their Wrongs and Claims,* was published in 1883. Born in Nevada, Winnemucca recounted her life as the daughter of the Piute chief, a position she took over at age 21, and her experiences dealing with federal Indian policies.

On lecture tours, she strove to dispel popular notions that Indians were uncivilized savages and to educate white audiences, government officials, and even President Hayes about the true situation of native peoples. Her focus on mutual understanding angered some of her tribe but also won support, especially among leading feminists of her era.

OUR NATIVE TONGUE

"Not a Chinaman's Chance"

In 1882 Congress passed the only immigration law in U.S. history to discriminate against a race of people. The Chinese Exclusion Act—a response to often violent public protest over increasing numbers of Chinese migrants—forbade any immigration from China, giving rise to the use of "not a Chinaman's chance" to refer to any impossible task.

By 1924 all Asian migration except from the Philippines was prohibited, and Asians already in the country were denied access to citizenship as well as the right to own property or marry Caucasians. This wall of racism didn't crack until World War II, when the United States and China allied against Japan.

BOOM, BUST, BOOM YEARS

From the Gilded Age through the Great Depression and World War II, the American Dream took a wild roller-coaster ride of thrilling highs and devastating plunges.

MARK TWAIN NAMES AN AGE

Twain's acute sense of the ridiculous, combined with his outrage at the rampant collusion of politicians and robber barons, led him to co-author, with his good friend Charles Dudley Warner, a satirical novel about vile corruption in high places. Published in 1873, *The Gilded Age* was not one of Twain's best efforts, but his title almost immediately caught on as the name for a period noted for its wretched excesses and *nouveau riche* sensibilities.

MRS. O'LEARY'S COW PLEADS INNOCENT

On the evening of Sunday, October 8, 1871, a fire broke out in the barn behind the O'Leary family's Chicago house. The flames spread quickly, and over the course of two days, the fire destroyed more than 2,000 acres of the densely populated city, including the central business district. Fatalities are estimated at 250; 100,000 people lost their homes and businesses. And Mrs. O'Leary, who kept several cows and sold milk to her neighbors, took all the heat. Even as the fire raged, rumors were circulating that Mrs. O'Leary had been in the barn when her cow kicked a lantern into the hay, though in fact the lady and her husband were in bed.

Whatever sparked the fire, investigators blamed extremely dry conditions (Chicago hadn't seen rain since July), strong winds,

Our Deadly Epidemics and Natural Disasters

Measured by loss of lives, this list comprises the four deadliest U.S. epidemics plus our worst natural disasters by type.

1918 Spanish influenza (nationwide)		500,000+ fatalities
1878 Yellow fever (lower Mississippi Valley)		13,000+
1853 Yellow fever (New Orleans)		7,790
1916 Polio (nationwide)		7,000+
1900 Hurricane: Galveston, Texas		Est. 6,000–8,000
1906 Earthquake: San Francisco	Est. 700–3,000 (dead or missing)	
1889 Flood: Johnstown, Pennsylvania		Est. 2,200
1871 Fire: Peshtigo, Wisconsin forest fire		Est. 1,500
1825 Tornado: Tri-State (Illinois, Indiana, Missouri)		689
1888 Snowstorm: East Coast Blizzard		400

wooden construction that included wooden streets and sidewalks, and the slow response of overworked firefighters. Yet the cow story wouldn't die, and the O'Leary family eventually left Chicago.

THE FRONTIER IS NOW CLOSED

Rarely does a historian make history. But that's what a young professor from the University of Wisconsin did in Chicago in 1893. Frederick Jackson Turner began a scholarly presentation by citing the 1890 census, which essentially declared the American frontier defunct. Turner then delivered his analysis that continuously expanding frontier settlement had always determined America's character, social as well as geographic and political. Turner concluded by asking how the closing of the frontier would affect the country's future—an important question at a time when American imperialism was a hot-button issue and people were wondering if "Manifest Destiny" meant spreading American power into the Caribbean, the Pacific, and other parts of the Americas.

Ignored at first, Turner's "frontier thesis" became one of the pivotal theories of the 20th century. It was clearly on John F. Kennedy's mind when he accepted the Democratic presidential nomination in 1960: " ... we stand today on the edge of a New Frontier ... a frontier of unknown opportunities and perils—a frontier of unfulfilled hopes and threats."

DEPOSING A PACIFIC QUEEN

Queen Liliuokalani ascended the Hawaiian throne after the death of her brother, King Kalakaua, in 1891. Well educated and widely traveled, the queen opposed her late brother's policy of transferring power, including control of Pearl Harbor, to American business interests. Her "Hawaii for Hawaiians" opposition to U.S. annexation prompted a bloodless *coup d'état* led by Stanford Dole, who represented the island's sugar growers, and abetted by the American ambassador.

President Cleveland sent a fact-finding mission to the islands and then ordered that Liliuokalani be restored. But the businessmen were already in control, and the former kingdom was annexed as a territory in 1900, with Dole its first governor. Based on official reports from the time, the U.S. Congress formally recognized the injustice in a 1993 joint resolution apologizing to the people of Hawaii.

HEARST STIRS THE CUBA POT

On February 15, 1898, the USS *Maine,* anchored in Havana Harbor, blew up and sank, costing the lives of 266 American sailors. Despite indications that the explosion might have been accidental, William Randolph Hearst, powerful publisher of the *New York Journal,* decided that Spanish colonial authorities in Cuba had deliberately attacked the battleship.

A Navy court at the time (and several later investigations) concluded that the *Maine,* which had entered the harbor illegally, most likely struck a mine. The Navy laid no blame on specific parties. Ignoring the official findings and his own reporters in Cuba, Hearst used sensational stories and lurid headlines to stoke a public frenzy. The clamor for war drowned out calmer voices, even after Spain made peaceful overtures. Hearst won the day when the United States and Spain declared war on each other in April.

LOOKING FOR MR. GOOD GOVERNMENT

By the 1880s the railroad trusts controlled Washington, and just about every city and town had its Tammany Hall–style political machine. Graft and corruption were so pervasive that ordinary citizens banded together in "good government" groups, bringing many into the larger Progressive reform movement. In 1912 Wisconsin's Senator Robert M. La Follette, a fervent enemy of the railroad combines, was instrumental in founding the National Progressive Republican League. The League supported direct election of U.S. senators; public primaries; initiative, referendum, and recall; and strong "corrupt practices" legislation—all aimed at restoring power to "We, the People."

But the Progressive goal of winning the White House was not to be: "Fighting Bob" La Follette's Progressive following was gutted by Teddy Roosevelt's "Bull Moose" campaign, and both candidates, as well as the incumbent, President Taft, were beaten by Woodrow Wilson.

OUR NATIVE TONGUE

The Yellow Kid

The term "yellow journalism"—the sensational, mawkish, aggressive bad boy of the press—was coined in 1897 by New York editor Ervin Wardman. Disgusted by the screaming headlines and shameless pandering of Hearst's *New York Journal* and Joseph Pulitzer's *New York World,* Wardman found a metaphor in the Yellow Kid, a bizarre street urchin who starred in the *World's* Hogan's Alley comic strip. Color printing was being introduced in newspapers, and the bald, jug-eared, two-toothed Kid was always clad in a yellow nightshirt.

The cartoon, drawn by Richard F. Outcault, was very popular and often crass, just like "yellow journalism." The Yellow Kid's fame faded after the Spanish-American War, in part because the color yellow had become negatively associated with both the Spanish flag and yellow fever.

THE TAX MAN COMETH

By the turn of the 20th century, an income tax had broad support among social reformers, unionists, Progressives, and average working people as the fairest way to bridge the country's widening gap between rich and poor.

Ratified in 1913, the Sixteenth Amendment gave birth to our modern progressive income tax system, complete with Form 1040. The initial rates ranged from just 1 percent on annual incomes over $3,000 to 7 percent on earnings above $500,000, after deductions, and less than 1 percent of Americans had to pay. The highest marginal rates came during the period from World War II to the Korean War—peaking at 92 percent in 1952 and 1953.

A CONGRESSWOMAN VOTES HER CONSCIENCE

In 1916 Janette Rankin of Montana became the first woman elected to Congress. Rankin, a lifelong advocate for international peace, lost her seat after she voted, with 55 male colleagues, against going to war with Germany in 1917. Twenty years later, she ran for Congress again and won. Fate intervened once more in December 1941, when, with tears in her eyes, she was the only member of Congress to vote against America's entry into World War II.

MENCKEN REPORTS THE MONEY TRIAL

In July 1925 John Thomas Scopes, a young substitute teacher, was tried for teaching evolution to the children of Dayton—a violation of Tennessee's newly passed Butler Law. As *Baltimore Sun* columnist H. L. Mencken pointed out, it was a show trial staged by local boosters to publicize their rural community. Mencken made no pretense of objectivity, writing bilious reports of the "Tennessee buffoonery" and "the old mountebank" William Jennings Bryant, who joined the prosecution team (and died five days after the verdict was rendered).

Then Mencken suddenly left "the Coca-Cola belt" early, missing defense attorney Clarence Darrow's famous confrontation with Bryant. Menken's writings suggest that it wasn't as easy to lampoon the citizens of Dayton ("a country town full of charm and beauty") as he'd expected.

THE REAL EFFECTS OF PROHIBITION

The failure of the Eighteenth Amendment, which prohibited the manufacture, distribution, and sale of alcohol, is often misunderstood. Between 1919 and 1933—the Amendment's life span—alcohol consumption declined significantly. But crime and violence increased, largely because millions of otherwise law-abiding Americans chose to defy this particular law.

Organized crime flourished in urban areas, where mobsters like Al Capone trafficked in alcohol, gambling, drugs, and prostitution. Liquor was smuggled from Canada, Mexico, and the Caribbean, and homemade hooch was available everywhere.

The federal government lacked the human resources to enforce the law; local and state authorities, from small-town sheriffs to high-court judges, were easily bought off or intimidated. The corruption of the culture was so widespread that even dedicated temperance advocates lobbied for the Twenty-First Amendment, which repealed Prohibition.

Scram! It's Izzy and Moe!

The intrepid G-men who raided speakeasies, smashed stills, and shot it out with rum runners during Prohibition were not from the FBI. They were agents of the Prohibition Bureau, created by the 1919 Volstead Act to enforce the Eighteenth Amendment.

The best known of these "prohis" (aka "dry agents") was Elliott Ness, who went after the Chicago mob. But the most successful were Isadore "Izzy" Einstein and Moe Smith, a dynamic duo who busted Manhattan speakeasies from 1920 to 1925. Celebrated for their quick wits, cunning ruses, and clever disguises, the pair accumulated the Prohibition Bureau's highest number of arrests (4,392) and best conviction record before they were rudely dismissed from the service, apparently for getting better press coverage than their superiors.

SINGING AND SWINGING THROUGH THE BAD OLD DAYS

After the Great Depression hit, Americans found comfort in popular music and movies. Even down-on-their-luck families got a lift seeing Ginger Rogers belt out "We're in the Money" ("Old Man Depression you are through, you done us wrong") and felt a lump in their throats as they watched Busby Berkeley's lavish dance number "Remember My Forgotten Man," both in *Gold Diggers* of 1933. With a radio or record player, folks could catch Bing Crosby's version of "Brother, Can You Spare a Dime?" or Woody Guthrie's "(If You Ain't Got the) Do Re Mi" (slang for money in the 1920s and '30s).

Recognizing that hard economic times call for hope and fantasy, the film, broadcast, and recording industries actually made "do re mi" during the Depression.

ROUTING THE "BONUS ARMY"

With the Depression deepening, some 20,000 unemployed World War I veterans, calling themselves the Bonus Expeditionary Force, came to Washington in 1932, vowing to stay until Congress handed over bonus checks promised in 1924. The bonuses—about $1,000 per man—weren't due until 1945, but vets contended that hard times called for an early dispersal.

They set up well-organized, orderly tent cities, and President Herbert Hoover instructed police to handle the situation with care. But after the Senate rejected a bill to pay the bonuses, Hoover ordered his military Chief of Staff, General Douglas MacArthur, to remove the squatters.

Exceeding his orders, MacArthur brought in armed infantry and cavalry, tanks, machine guns, and tear gas. In the rout, two veterans and an infant died and about a thousand protesters were injured. The public was enraged by MacArthur's overreaction, and Hoover's last hope of reelection went up in smoke.

THE STAY OUT MOVEMENT

Even after Hitler invaded Poland, American opposition to entering World War II remained strong. The most prominent isolationist organization was the America First Committee, launched in 1940 by Yale law student Charles Stuart and friends including Gerald Ford, future president, and Potter Stewart, future Supreme Court justice. The power came from businessmen including Robert E. Wood, head of Sears Roebuck, and Sterling Morton of Morton Salt.

Presidential Fact File

As leaders U.S. presidents have been a mixed lot, but however great or poor their performance in office, they've all been interesting in their own way. Some bits and pieces about our heads of state:

Tallest: Abraham Lincoln, 6'4"

Shortest: James Madison, 5'4", a bit under average at the time

Largest: William Howard Taft, 6'2" and 330 pounds

Shortest Time in Office: William Henry Harrison, 33 days (He died of pneumonia after catching cold during his inauguration.)

Longest Time in Office: Franklin Roosevelt, 12 years and 39 days

Presidents by a Landslide: Only Warren Harding, Franklin Roosevelt, Lyndon Johnson, and Richard Nixon were elected with 60 percent or more of the popular vote.

Born on July 4: Calvin Coolidge in 1872

Died on July 4: Thomas Jefferson and John Adams in 1826; James Monroe in 1831

First President Not Born a British Citizen: Martin Van Buren, born in 1782

First President Born in a Hospital: Jimmy Carter

Suffered Serious Illness in Secret: Chester A. Arthur (Bright's disease); Grover Cleveland (mouth cancer); John F. Kennedy (Addison's disease). Franklin Roosevelt's polio was known but not publicized. Woodrow Wilson suffered several strokes, and the severity of his condition was hidden until he left office.

Assassinated in Office: Abraham Lincoln, James Garfield, William McKinley, John F. Kennedy

Died in Office: William Henry Harrison, Zachary Taylor, Warren Harding

Targets of Failed Assassination Attempts: Andrew Jackson, Theodore Roosevelt, Franklin Roosevelt, Harry Truman, Gerald Ford, Ronald Reagan

Bachelor Presidents: James Buchanan, Grover Cleveland

Married in the White House: Cleveland, age 48, married 21-year-old

Frances ("Frankie") Folsom in a simple ceremony in the Blue Room. Many Washington insiders were shocked, not by the age difference but because they thought the President had been courting her mother.

Presidents Who Were Also Kin: John Adams and John Quincy Adams (father/son); George H. W. Bush and George W. Bush (father/son); William Henry Harrison and Benjamin Harrison (grandfather/grandson); Theodore Roosevelt and Franklin Roosevelt (cousins)

Most Exotic White House Pet: Thomas Jefferson's grizzly bear, the gift of Lewis and Clark. Runner-up: the Taft children's alligators

First President Born Outside the Contiguous States: Barack Obama, born in Hawaii in 1961.

Only Adopted President: Gerald Ford, though a number of presidents were reared by relatives or stepparents.

Presidential Parties: From 1788 to 2009 there have been 19 Republican presidents, 14 Democrats, 4 Whigs, 3 Democratic-Republicans (or Jeffersonian-Democrats), and 2 Federalists (Washington and John Adams, though Washington didn't have an official party affiliation).

Only President Elected Unanimously by the Electoral College: George Washington. His successor, John Adams, fell one vote short of unanimity when an elector held out in order to preserve Washington's perfect record.

First President to Refuse a Second Term: James K. Polk

Only Unelected President: Gerald Ford was not elected president or vice president. He was appointed vice president by Richard Nixon and assumed the presidency when Nixon resigned.

Only President to Sit on the Supreme Court: William Howard Taft was appointed Chief Justice after leaving the White House.

Number of Presidents Who Owned Slaves: 12

Only President to Win a Pulitzer Prize: John Kennedy for *Profiles in Courage*.

First President to Throw the First Baseball: Taft opened the 1910 baseball season by throwing out the first pitch (Washington Senators versus Philadelphia Athletics).

An estimated 800,000 members ranged from socialist Norman Thomas to silent film queen Lillian Gish. But the real star was aviator Charles A. Lindbergh, who stumped the country for the cause and, during a Des Moines, Iowa appearance, nearly destroyed his personal reputation with comments interpreted by some as anti-Semitic.

The Committee disbanded immediately after the December 1941 attack on Pearl Harbor, and most members signed up to support their nation at war.

FDR AND THE RADIO

Thanks to radio, Franklin Roosevelt was the first president able to communicate directly and regularly with the American people. Millions tuned in to his "fireside chats"—30 evening broadcasts during the Depression and World War II. Opening with his signature "Good evening, friends," he spoke in a calm, reassuring manner even as he informed his listeners of the difficulties that lay ahead.

Broadcast technology has vastly improved since those early, scratchy radio days, but no subsequent president has equaled FDR's skill at personalizing electronic communication, though John F. Kennedy's witty televised press conferences and Ronald Reagan's best speeches came close.

MODERN TIMES

After World War II we weathered the Cold War,
became the world's only superpower, and saw the
Founders' ideals realized with the election of the
nation's first African American president.

"CANDY BOMBERS" OVER BERLIN

The 1948 to 1949 Soviet blockade of eastern Berlin was the first
major international crisis after World War II. The Allies responded
by airlifting tons of food and supplies. Flying cargo planes into the
besieged zone from Templehof air base, U.S. Air Force Colonel Gail
Halvorsen began to drop candy, chewing gum, and other treats—
attached to parachutes made from handkerchiefs—to the German
children below. Other pilots followed his lead, and with Air Force
approval, the candy drops were dubbed "Operation Little Vittles."

Begun as a singular gesture of goodwill, the drops were a great
morale booster for Berliners. Two decades after the airlift, Halvorsen
returned to Berlin, this time as commander of the Templehof base.

IKE'S ROADS TO EVERYWHERE

Dwight Eisenhower never forgot his 1919 experience as a young
Army officer participating in the military's first cross-country motor
caravan—traveling five miles an hour over terrible roads. The drive
from Washington to San Francisco took 62 days. Good roads were in
such short supply that a national highway network proposed during
the New Deal gained wide public support, but was shelved during
World War II.

As president, Eisenhower, inspired now by the German Autobahn, made modern highways a top priority. After a series of preliminary funding bills and a great deal of negotiation, Congress passed and Ike signed the Federal-Aid Highway Act of 1956. The Ohio-to-California segment of today's I-80, one of the longest roads in our interstate system, closely follows the military convoy route that Eisenhower traveled in 1919.

OUR NATIVE TONGUE

Atomic Slang

The Cold War added more than a hint of paranoia to everyday speech in the 1950s and '60s. Teens, who grew up watching nuclear bomb tests on TV, described a great party as a *blast* (their parents would have said *bash* or *ball)* and a very popular person as *radioactive*. A super smart kid might be a *brainiac* (likely a play on ENIAC, the "Giant Brain" computer introduced by the Army in 1946), but simple tasks weren't *rocket science.*

A businessman who went *ballistic* (exploded like a ballistic missile) and demanded *more bang for the buck* (a cost-benefit expression applied to spending on nuclear weapons) could drown his sorrows by getting *bombed* (late '50s slang for seriously inebriated) on potent *atomic cocktails* and wind up with an *atom-splitter* of a hangover.

To a *beatnik* or *peacenik* (derived from Sputnik), all authority was *Big Brother* (from George Orwell's *1984*, published in 1949) and all conformists were *brainwashed* (psychological torture and indoctrination attributed to the Chinese) by the system.

The first use of the term *Cold War* is often attributed to a 1947 speech by financier and presidential adviser Bernard Baruch, but the honor goes to Orwell, who wrote of "a permanent state of 'cold war'" in his 1945 essay "You and the Atomic Bomb."

THE STRATEGIST OF DESEGREGATION

If any one person deserves credit for the long struggle to overthrow legal segregation, it's Charles Hamilton Houston. A graduate of Amherst College and Yale Law School, Houston led the fight for accreditation of black law schools and formulated the strategy of attacking *Plessy v. Ferguson* (the 1898 Supreme Court decision establishing "separate but equal" as the law of the land) via cases involving education.

He taught and mentored the NAACP lawyers, including Thurgood Marshall, who finally shattered "separate but equal" when they won the landmark *Brown v. Board of Education* case in 1954. Charlie Houston, a workaholic of the best kind, died in 1950, before he could taste the fruits of his labors or see Marshall appointed the first black justice of the Supreme Court.

HOW NOT TO DUMP A DICTATOR

Details of "Operation Mongoose" and "Operation Northwoods," two CIA plans to kill or overthrow Cuban leader Fidel Castro in the early 1960s, were slow in reaching the public. The secret program—a joint effort of the Justice and Defense Departments and personally overseen by Robert Kennedy—included some ideas that were patently ridiculous, like killing Castro with an exploding cigar. Others involved spreading false rumors in Cuba, such as one in which Castro planned to take all Cuban children away from their parents.

More serious suggestions involved staging fake terrorist attacks, with the possibility of real casualties, in Miami or at Guantanamo Bay to arouse public fury and allow the United States to invade Cuba with impunity. Whether President Kennedy knew about these James Bond–esque plots isn't known.

1968: A SEASON OF PROTEST

Many people thought the United States was on the verge of anarchy during the summer of 1968: Campus protests, including the shutdown of Columbia University, were the norm. Martin Luther King Jr. was assassinated in April, precipitating urban riots nationwide. A feminist radical nearly killed Pop artist Andy Warhol on June 3. Two days later, Robert F. Kennedy was shot in Los Angeles, minutes after winning the California Democratic primary; he died the next day. Vietnam War protestors at the Democratic National Convention were beaten by Chicago police, and televised images of the riots doomed Democratic hopes of retaining the White House.

But there were good moments. The S&P 500 index closed above 100 for the first time. The Beatles created Apple Records. Mattel introduced Hot Wheels. And the Medal of Honor was awarded posthumously to James Anderson Jr. for his heroic action "above and beyond the call of duty" during a firefight near Cam Lo in Vietnam. PFC Anderson, who died saving fellow Marines from an enemy grenade, was the first African American to receive the nation's highest tribute.

THE MOON ROCKS! OR NOT

Soon after Neil Armstrong, Edwin "Buzz" Aldrin, and Michael Collins returned from their epic *Apollo 11* journey to the moon, public attention turned to what they brought back. Scientists studying the small collection of lunar rocks, soil, and dust were harassed and badgered until NASA announced a display of specimens at the Smithsonian Institute. Thousands lined up, eager for a first peek, but the samples were, well, just rocks.

More interesting is what the astronauts had left on the moon: a disk with the recorded words of four U.S. presidents, the leaders of 72 nations, and Pope Paul VI; a "We Came in Peace" plaque;

and the shoulder patches and medals of the five American astronauts and Soviet cosmonauts who had died serving in their nations' space programs.

PING-PONG POLITICS, BUT WHO WON?

It's been said that only Nixon could go to China (as he did in 1972). First, however, were America's table tennis champions, who received a surprise invitation to compete against their Chinese counterparts in April 1971. Accompanied by 10 foreign journalists, they were the first American group admitted to China since 1949.

The U.S. players lost their exhibition games but charmed their hosts, especially Premier Chou En-lai, who milked every drop of goodwill from the event. The Americans' "ping pong diplomacy" and a follow-up U.S. tour by a Chinese team helped thaw relations with the People's Republic.

A DUST-UP IN THE CARIBBEAN

Not many Americans had heard of the tiny Caribbean island of Granada when the U.S. military invaded it on October 25, 1983. Twelve days earlier, Granada's socialist government had been overthrown, and President Ronald Reagan's administration, fearing the island was already too cozy with Fidel Castro's Cuba, reacted with overwhelming force, in spite of opposition from Great Britain, Granada's former colonial power.

The public rationale was to protect Americans on the island, including 800 medical students. For those who remember Operation Urgent Fury, the real reasons for sending 8,000 men to conquer the little nation are still open to debate.

CONTROVERSIAL WAR, CONTROVERSIAL MONUMENT

When a 21-year-old Yale undergraduate, Maya Ying Lin, was selected to memorialize America's more than 58,000 military personnel lost in the Vietnam War, the choice was immediately challenged. Many people didn't get Lin's stark, nonfigurative design, and some objected to her Asian heritage, although she was born and raised in Ohio. Since the 1982 dedication, however, the black granite wall of names on the Washington Mall has become one of the country's most visited and beloved memorials.

To quiet the controversy, in 1984 a more traditional bronze grouping, "Three Servicemen," was installed not far from the Vietnam Veterans Memorial wall. Another figurative bronze, honoring the women who served in the war, was added in 1993.

DIDN'T HAPPEN!

The Gulf of Tonkin Attack

On August 2, 1964, the battleship USS *Maddox,* patrolling international waters off the coast of North Vietnam, was attacked by three P-T boats, causing little damage. A second attack on the *Maddox* and the USS *Turner Joy* was reported on August 4, and the United States retaliated with air strikes on North Vietnamese port facilities. On August 7, Congress passed the Tonkin Gulf Resolution, empowering President Lyndon Johnson to use military force as he saw fit.

In 2005 declassified documents released by the National Security Council confirmed what historians had suspected for years—the August 4 attack had not happened. Yet this second reported incident had expedited Congress's action and led directly to major escalation of the Vietnam War.

THE COLD WAR ENDS

In February 1992, President George H. W. Bush and Russian President Boris Yeltsin met at Camp David in Maryland to discuss common concerns following the fall of the Berlin Wall and the collapse of the Soviet Union. Many failed to notice that the two world leaders also declared the Cold War officially over, ending almost a half century of mutual hostility. Their joint declaration pledged a new relationship "founded on mutual trust and respect and a common commitment to democracy and economic freedom."

Though little else was accomplished at the meeting, it did shore up Yeltsin's still shaky status as a world leader.

INAUGURATION '09: THE PROMISE FULFILLED

When Barack Obama took his oath of office in the blustery cold wind of January 21, 2009, it was a time for reflection not only on his history-making presidency but also on the setting, the U.S. Capitol. On a warm September day in 1793, President Washington stood on the same site for the laying of the Capitol's cornerstone, a large piece of local granite most likely quarried and cut by black slaves.

No one knows the exact number of slaves who worked on the Capitol's construction between 1793 and its completion in 1826. We do know that "Negro hires"—stone and wood workers, bricklayers, roofers, timber sawers and carpenters, plasterers, painters—made up a large portion of the crews supplied by slave-owning contractors. Few slave names were listed in billing records. Still, they were remembered as the country's first African American president took office on the Capitol steps more than 200 years after their work began.

Sailing Ships to Space Stations

Our Industry and Innovations

The solid work ethic of the American people dates from our earliest days, and the nation's can-do spirit spawned legions of innovators. Immigrants such as Alexander Graham Bell and John Jacob Astor also did their part to push the United States to the forefront of industry, commerce, and invention. As time went on, new technologies put astronauts in outer space and computers in our homes—machines that would connect us to the world with little more than the click of a mouse.

INDUSTRY'S SECOND WAVE

IN ENGLAND THE ARRIVAL OF THE STEAM ENGINE (1776)
STARTED THE INDUSTRIAL REVOLUTION, AND A SECOND WAVE
SOON BEGAN TO SWELL ACROSS THE POND.

IN-YOUR-FACE PRODUCTION IN THE COLONIES

Colonist Mark Bird built Hopewell Furnace in Pennsylvania in 1771, five years before James Watt's steam engine jump-started the industrial revolution in Europe. Stoves were its most profitable items, but the furnace also cast machinery, grates, kettles, and other objects—despite England's Act of 1750, which prohibited the manufacture of finished iron products in the Colonies. Flaunting such rules was good sport for patriots, and for Bird and many of his customers, "Buy British" just didn't fly.

THE "SMUGGLER" WHO STARTED IT ALL

Starting at age 14, Samuel Slater apprenticed with a textile technology pioneer and learned the trade secrets the British religiously kept from American manufacturers. Lured to New England in 1789 by a reward for the invention of a machine to make "cotton rollers," Slater memorized the components of the water-powered spinning frame that gave the British the competitive edge and "smuggled" it through customs in his head. (Slater was known for his excellent memory.)

The mill he transformed in Pawtucket, Rhode Island, in 1793 spun the first cotton yarn in America and became the prototype for thousands of mills over the next century—the reason Slater came to be known as the "Father of American Manufactures."

SHIPPING MAKES NEW YORK

Shipping was already going great guns in New York Harbor when Jeremiah Thompson and three other Quaker merchants started the first shipping line the world had ever seen. In January 1818 the ships of the Black Ball Line began leaving for Liverpool at a specified time each month, whether empty or full. Previously, a ship's departure time had depended on how long it took to assemble a crew, load enough cargo to make the voyage worthwhile, or wait for good weather.

This so-called packet service spawned a host of imitators and flourished so rapidly that shipping lines became commonplace, taking the question of "when?" out of sea transport and giving our language a new expression—on time.

JOHN JACOB ASTOR: OUR FIRST MILLIONAIRE

Lewis & Clark had scarcely returned home from their expedition when John Jacob Astor, a German immigrant of humble birth, founded the Pacific Fur Company in 1810 and wasted no time traveling from New York to the Columbia River to establish the first American trading post.

In a day when beaver fur was as good as gold, Astor became the country's first millionaire—not least because he branched out in real estate and soon owned whole blocks in upper Manhattan, the land beneath Times Square, and much of the Lower East Side.

ANDREW CARNEGIE: WORLD'S RICHEST MAN

The son of financially strapped immigrants from Scotland, 12-year-old Andrew Carnegie took a job as a bobbin boy in a textile mill, earning $1.20 a week. Fifty-three years later, in 1901, he sold the steel company he founded and became the world's richest man. Carnegie chose to give away his fortune, and in his book *The*

Cassie Chadwick: Carnegie's "Daughter"

A born swindler, Ohioan Elizabeth Bigley temporarily suspended her serial deceptions so she could snag a Dr. Chadwick of Cleveland. It was then that newly minted "Cassie" Chadwick began to think big.

Starting in 1897 Chadwick posed as Andrew Carnegie's illegitimate daughter so convincingly that local banks lent her up to $20 million. When the scam collapsed in 1904, the woman who had been called Cleveland's "society queen" fled to New York, where a police detective arrested her and found she was wearing a money belt stuffed with more than $100,000.

Gospel of Wealth argued that the rich have an obligation to serve as stewards for society. By 1911 he had distributed 90 percent of his money, funding colleges and universities and building libraries in cities and towns—1,689 libraries in the United States and some 850 in other countries.

J. P. MORGAN: FINANCIER, STARGAZER

John Pierpont Morgan dominated finance for much of the 19th century, pulling the strings in railroads, shipping, and manufacturing both in the United States and overseas. In 1902 he suffered a rare business defeat when he wasn't allowed to build a tunnel beneath London to compete with the subway system known as the Tube.

Morgan's passion for collecting art and rare books is well known, but he was also keen on astrology. He belonged to a secret society called the Zodiac of the Twelve—in which each member took a different astrological sign and went by Brother Aries, Brother Pisces, and so on. In Midtown Manhattan's Morgan Library, the financier's former home, numerous zodiacal references are hidden in the ceiling murals and elsewhere. The library also houses a wealth of material on the zodiac and the constellations.

JOHN D. ROCKEFELLER: FROM MONOPOLIST TO PHILANTHROPIST

The son of an upstate New York quack who sold cures for "cancer" at $25 a pop, John D. Rockefeller was a businessman from the start. In 1851 the 12-year-old Rockefeller lent $50 he earned working for neighbors to a local farmer at 7 percent interest—and once it was paid back, he surely thought to himself, "This is easy."

The founder of Standard Oil, which he built into America's first giant monopoly, was no hero in the eyes of the public. But Rockefeller found redemption by devoting himself to philanthropy in the last 40 years of his life. His descendants followed suit and spread the wealth by way of their charitable foundations.

HENRY FORD: FATHER OF MASS PRODUCTION

Henry Ford didn't invent the automobile, but he knew how to sell his new "horseless carriage" like nobody's business. The conveyor-belt assembly line Ford developed in the early 1900s reduced production costs by reducing labor time; it took only 93 minutes to assemble a Model T Ford. In 1908 the first Model Ts that rolled off the assembly line sold for $850 and—in a textbook example of the law of supply and demand—the 1916 price was $350.

KINGS OF THE RAILS

Railroad moguls drove much of the economic development in the 19th century, and they amassed great fortunes in the process. The biggest movers and shakers included:

Cornelius Vanderbilt, who before he founded the New York Central and Hudson River railroads, owned 100 steamships and was given the nickname "Commodore"

Jay Gould, an unscrupulous and very rich player who gained control of four western railroads, including Union Pacific

Edward Henry Harriman, who made his first fortune on Wall Street and his second when he seized control of the Union Pacific Railroad during the Panic of 1893

Leland Stanford, Collis P. Huntington, Mark Hopkins, and Charles Crocker ("The Big Four"), Easterners who made their fortunes in the West before banding together to build the Central Pacific Railroad.

EARLY ENVIRONMENTAL STIRRINGS

The seeds of the environmental movement were planted during the second industrial revolution by John Muir, the Yosemite dweller who became one of the nation's first conservationists and founded the Sierra Club in 1892. Conservation of nature was also the focus of the National Audubon Society (1905).

As industrial pollution became a threat, these two organizations added the fight for clean air and a healthy environment to their agenda. Today they coexist with antipollution nonprofits, such as the Environmental Defense Fund (1967) and The Climate Project, founded by Al Gore in 2006.

Robber Barons or Captains of Industry?

The richest industrialists were dubbed robber barons because it was assumed (and often rightly) that at least a portion of their fortunes came from under-handed business practices. But Rockefeller and his kind bequeathed so much to charity and society at large that the good ultimately outweighed the bad.

Some historians hold up "captains of industry" as the more fair-minded label—not that most of the men in question ever heard the more pejorative term. Robber baron—possibly derived from the medieval German lords who charged exorbitant tolls to ships plying the Rhine River—didn't gain real currency until the throes of the Great Depression, when economic analyst Matthew Josephson wrote the best-selling book *The Robber Barons: The Great American Capitalists, 1861–1900.*

THE WORLD OF WORK

FROM COLONIAL DAYS ONWARD, AMERICANS TOILED AS FARM
WORKERS, TRADESMEN, OR MERCHANTS—BUT THE NATURE OF
LABOR OF ANY STRIPE WAS IN FOR A BIG CHANGE.

"OUR PRINCIPAL WEALTH . . . CONSISTETH IN SERVANTS."

So wrote John Pory, secretary of Virginia, to an official of the
Virginia Company in 1619. When tobacco was the lifeblood of the
colony, there weren't enough workers to cultivate and harvest the
labor-intensive plant. The answer lay in indentured servants from
Europe, who labored for four or five years in exchange for passage,
food, shelter, and perhaps a land grant. Likewise, many of the first
slaves transported to Virginia were freed once their service ended.

Later in the 17th century and through much of the 18th century,
the need for workers was such that well over half of the colonists in
America had arrived as indentured servants. Immigration records tell
the story: Between 1773 and 1776, servants accounted for 96 percent
of English immigrants to Virginia and Maryland; 61 percent to New
York and Pennsylvania; 20 percent to the Carolinas and Georgia; and
2 percent to New England, due to its limited agriculture.

ENTER THE MINIMUM WAGE

Australia and New Zealand did it in the 1890s, and Great Britain
followed in 1909. Massachusetts enacted it for women and children
in 1912, but the United States as a whole took another 26 years
to get behind the minimum wage. The Fair Labor Standards Act
of 1938 set the first base hourly wage for most American workers:

25 cents—about $3.80 in real dollars (today's money). The minimum wage peaked in 1968 at $9.47 in real dollars.

WHEN SALESMEN MADE HOUSE CALLS

Until the mid-1900s America's traveling salesmen hawked goods door to door. From the Fuller Brush man (the icon of the trade) to college kids selling encyclopedias, Bibles, and magazines, commercial foot soldiers blanketed the nation and were often treated as welcome guests.

An example of the efficacy of house calls: The Hoover Suction Sweeper Company, the Ohio manufacturer of the first vacuum cleaner, sold its products in stores but owed its success to the door-to-door salesmen who demonstrated the Hoover in people's homes.

THE PULLMAN STRIKE: SHOCK AND AWE

George Pullman, the leading manufacturer of railroad cars, built a namesake model town for his workers on the edge of Chicago. But he cut their wages by 25 percent during the Panic of 1893. In May 1884 the workers began to strike, and unions in 27 states staged sympathy strikes at the behest of Eugene Debs, head of the Railway Workers Union—one of the many labor unions showing new muscle.

When negotiations collapsed in early July, mayhem broke out in Chicago. Over three days of rioting, more than 1,000 railroad cars were destroyed, seven buildings on the grounds of the Chicago Exposition were burned down, and at least 13 people were killed—some by the National Guard troops called in to keep the peace.

Eighty-six years later, in 1970, the Chicago suburb of Pullman was made a National Historic Landmark.

A Brief History of Buying

Thanks to peddlers, many early Americans bought goods without leaving home. Almost three centuries later, we've come full circle in a way.

General stores. Typically boasting a porch with rocking chairs and an indoor wood-burning stove, these stores were stacked from floor to ceiling with goods of every sort. They sometimes served as the post office and a de facto community center.

Department stores. The first large store to group a variety of merchandise in different rooms was in Duxbury, Massachusetts: James T. Ford & Company, which opened in 1826. So-called department stores took a turn toward the grand when R. H. Macy & Co. opened in New York City in 1858.

Chain stores. The first store to open more than one outlet selling the same goods began doing business in 1859—the Great Atlantic & Pacific Tea Company (A & P) grocery store. Among the major players who followed suit were Woolworth's (1870) and J. C. Penney (1902).

Mail-order shopping. In 1862 Chicago merchant Aaron Montgomery Ward printed the first catalog, largely for farmers. In 1886 rival merchant R. W. Sears issued his own version, which by the turn of the century had grown into the Sears Roebuck catalog, selling more than 6,000 items of every stripe.

Shopping malls. The nation's first shopping mall—a set of retail buildings with interconnecting walkways—went up in 1922: Country Club Plaza, in Kansas City. The first enclosed mall—Southdale, in the Minneapolis suburb of Edina in 1956—was designed to help shoppers escape Minnesota's frigid weather.

Big-box stores. Sam Walton opened his first Wal-Mart discount store in Bentonville, Arkansas, in 1950 and had 10 more by 1962—the same year Kmart was founded. These and similar big-box retailers quickly spread across the land, leaving thousands of shuttered small-town businesses in their wake.

Online shopping. With the coming of eBay and similar Web sites in the early 1990s, Americans began to shop over the Internet from the comfort of home. Before you could say "Sales slump alert!" brick-and-mortar stores of every sort jumped on the electronic bandwagon.

ON THE FARM

THE AMERICAN ECONOMY RODE ON THE BACKS OF FARMERS UNTIL
THE SECOND INDUSTRIAL REVOLUTION SOWED THE SEEDS OF
MECHANIZED AGRICULTURE.

OUR FIRST CASH CROP

The first native Virginia tobacco was sold to England in 1614, and demand for the crop increased so heavily that agents for the growers brought over the first African slaves. In 1620 Virginia exported 40,000 pounds of tobacco, which became so essential to the economy that it was used as currency for the next 200 years.

Later in the century the bloom went off the *Nicotiana tabacum* rose. At a time when the English were saturated to the gills with tobacco from the Chesapeake colonies (Virginia and Maryland), the Navigation Act of 1660 forbade shipment of tobacco or tobacco products to anywhere but England or its colonies. The tobacco industry recovered, but its history would be one of ups and downs right into the 21st century.

ELIZA LUCAS'S INDIGO

Eliza Lucas was born in Antigua to British Army Lieutenant Colonel George Lucas and his wife, Anne. In 1738, when Eliza was 14, Lucas relocated the family to the South Carolina plantation he had inherited from his father.

The next year Lucas was recalled to Antigua when a conflict erupted between the English and Spanish (see the War of Jenkins' Ear, page 25), leaving the management of the 5,000-acre plantation to his capable teenage daughter. He also began to send seeds for Eliza to test in the rich South Carolina soil—among them indigo, the source of a deep blue dye.

The industrious Eliza saw her first indigo crop killed by a freeze, and it wasn't until 1744 that a bountiful harvest came in. Thereafter the exotic plant first cultivated in America by a young woman became a mainstay of the Southern colonies' economy.

Top Crops in the Colonies

In the 18th century the Middle Colonies were known as the breadbasket, though grains could be grown almost anywhere. Only New England, with its short growing season and rocky soils, had it tough when it came to farming.

The following crops were well suited to each region:

New England Colonies (New Hampshire, Massachusetts, Rhode Island, Connecticut)

- Flax (for making cloth)
- Hemp (for rope)

Middle Colonies (New York, New Jersey, Pennsylvania, Delaware)

- Wheat
- Oats
- Corn
- Rye
- Barley

Southern Colonies (Maryland, Virginia, North Carolina, South Carolina, Georgia)

- Tobacco
- Rice
- Indigo (for dye)

FARMING TRANSFORMED

Some 40 years after Eli Whitney invented the cotton gin and revived the cotton industry (see "The Machine That Made Cotton King," page 43), the horse-drawn reaper invented by Cyrus H. McCormick made the sickle and scythe tools of the past. Grain harvesting increased dramatically not only in the United States but throughout the world. McCormick's inventor father, Robert, tried unsuccessfully for 28 years to develop a horse-drawn reaper—and when he gave up and turned the project over to his son, Cyrus perfected the reaper in a mere year and a half.

In the 1850s blacksmith John Deere experimented with an old saw blade to develop the first cast-steel plow. The large plows he wrought could cut through the sticky Midwestern soil without clogging, and by 1855 John Deere's factory was selling more than 10,000 plows a year.

BARBED WIRE: PROVING THE POINT

Joseph F. Glidden, who invented barbed wire, had trouble selling skeptical farmers and ranchers on wire fencing. So in 1876 he sent his savvy associate John Gates around the country to prove the wire's worth.

Gate's MO was ingenious. In San Antonio, Texas, he erected a corral made of fence posts and barbed wire in a city plaza, then filled it with a borrowed herd of longhorn cattle. Much to the amazement of the cattlemen and farmers invited to the demonstration, the wire studded with sharp blades held when the cattle charged it and then drew back in shock. The upshot? Barbed wire sales jumped from less than 3 million pounds in 1876 to over 12 million in 1877.

BONANZA FARMS: LARGER THAN LIFE

Huge tracts of land in the fertile Red River Valley, between Minnesota and the Dakota Territory, were opened by private landowners for cultivation in the late 1870s. Much of the acreage was sold for next to nothing by the Northern Pacific Railroad, which had recently completed a link between the valley and the Great Lakes but went bankrupt in the Panic of 1873.

Some of these so-called bonanza farms were five times the size of Manhattan, and crews working one part of the farm might labor all season without laying eyes on those in another sector.

IOWAN SPARKS A GREEN REVOLUTION

In 1945 a joint project between the Mexican government and American philanthropies, including the Rockefeller and Ford foundations, sought to increase agricultural production by introducing new food plants and farming methods. One of the scientists on the project, Iowa-born agronomist Norman Borlaug, developed a strain of dwarf spring wheat that produced such high yields that it transformed agriculture in North America and around the world.

In 1968 William Gaud, a former director of the United States Agency for International Development, was the first to use the term "green revolution" in relation to the project. As for Borlaug, he was awarded the 1970 Nobel Peace Prize for his groundbreaking work.

G. W. Carver and H. Ford: Fast Friends

George Washington Carver made his name in the South, but he made some of his most valued friends in the North—Henry Ford, for one. Carver, who in his days at the Tuskegee Institute in Alabama worked to prove that plants could be turned into plastics, fuel, and other products, caught Ford's attention when Ford donated money to Tuskegee in the late 1930s.

Ford had long been interested in developing biofuels, and the automobile mogul and the African American scientist began to explore the industrial uses of soybeans and other plants. The two went on to develop a warm friendship based on mutual admiration and respect.

ECONOMIC UPS AND DOWNS

OUR ECONOMY HAS SEEN GOOD TIMES AND BAD AND IS A FORCE
THAT ALTERNATELY GAINED STEAM AND SPUTTERED SINCE
WE BEGAN TRADING STOCKS IN 1792.

"CURB MARKET" TO "WALL STREET"

The New York Stock Exchange (NYSE) began doing business in 1792
after 24 New York City stockbrokers and merchants signed the Buttonwood Agreement, named for the buttonwood tree under which it
was signed. The stock exchange we know colloquially as Wall Street
was originally called the "curb market" because its brokers traded
outdoors on the sidewalk.

Today's NYSE (on Broad, not Wall, Street opened in April 1903
to great fanfare. The interior of the neoclassical edifice fits the bill,
made with marble walls soaring 72 feet to an ornate gilt ceiling.

WHAT PUT THE ROAR IN THE TWENTIES?

In the Roaring Twenties, Americans broke with the past as our
country became the richest in the world, mass production put an
unimaginable array of consumer goods on store shelves, and Victorian stuffiness gave way to a love of fads and fun.

Jazz provided the soundtrack as people flocked to movies and
danced to radio music, women shortened their hair and hemlines,
and men took pride in their sporty roadsters. People borrowed money
from banks like it was going out of style, and speakeasies flaunted
the strictures of Prohibition. Yet as the good times rolled, millions of
people lived below the poverty line of $2,000 per family.

THE REAL CAUSES OF THE GREAT DEPRESSION

The Depression hardly started with Black Thursday. The stock market crash of 1929 was only a reflection of underlying problems—one of them not being sunspots, as one theory holds. Among the causes were:

Uneven distribution of wealth. By the end of the decade, the richest 0.1 percent of families had a total income equal to that of the bottom 41 percent.

A farming slump. After World War I, farmers found themselves competing in an oversupplied international market, and agriculture fell into a depression in the early '20s.

The First Dow Jones Industrial Stocks

The Dow Jones Industrial Average was first calculated in the 1880s on the price per share of 12 companies. This initial list was published on May 26, 1896, and only one company—General Electric—remains in the portfolio today.

- American Cotton Oil
- American Sugar (now Domino Sugar)
- American Tobacco
- Chicago Gas
- Distilling and Cattle Feeding Company
- General Electric
- Laclede Gas
- National Lead (now NL Industries)
- North American (a utility holding company)
- Tennessee Coal & Iron
- United States Leather Company
- United States Rubber Company (now Uniroyal, Inc.)

Roosevelt's Depression-Era Alphabet

As FDR's New Deal agenda moved forward, Americans were swamped with programs designed to defeat the Depression by providing immediate relief and establishing long-term economic stability. These "alphabet agencies" included but were by no means limited to:

AAA   Agricultural Adjustment Administration

CAA   Civil Aeronautics Authority

CCC   Civilian Conservation Corps

FCA   Farm Credit Administration

FDIC   Federal Deposit Insurance Corporation

FHA   Federal Housing Authority

HOLC   Home Owners Loan Corporation

NLRB   National Labor Relations Board

NYA   National Youth Administration

SEC   Securities and Exchange Commission

SSB   Social Security Board

THE WPA DOES THE JOB

The Works Progress Administration (WPA) was the largest agency of the New Deal—the name President Franklin D. Roosevelt gave to a series of Depression recovery programs he initiated between 1933 and 1936 to provide work for the unemployed and reform business and financial practices. The WPA built or improved enough roads to circle the globe 24 times, enough bridges to connect New Orleans with Havana, 125,110 public buildings, 8,192 parks, 853 airports, and untold numbers of public art works.

The WPA companion agency, the Public Works Administration (PWA), launched major projects including Hoover Dam, Chicago's sewer system, and the aircraft carriers *Yorktown* and *Enterprise*.

Depressions of Times Past

The only thing new about economic depressions is their name: Until the mid–20th century they were called panics. Read on to see how some things never change.

Panic of 1819

The Bank of the United States, or BUS (a joint venture between the government and private investors), overextended credit to state banks but exercised little control. State banks in turn overextended credit to land speculators in the West and to Eastern business promoters. Unable to collect on their loans or pay BUS, many state banks collapsed and many properties in the West were foreclosed on. Despite the Public Land Act of 1820, which made land much easier to purchase, the depression in the West lasted until 1824.

Panic of 1837

Along with a decline in cotton prices, the immediate cause of this depression was the failure of several British banks, which precipitated the collapse of American banks. By May 1837 the federal government had lost $9 million in failed "pet banks," unregulated banks that encouraged speculation. The depression lasted into the mid-1840s and was particularly hard on cities. As a consequence, President Van Buren proposed creation of an independent U.S. Treasury.

Panic of 1857

While overbuilding of railroads and a downturn in Western land prices led to mortgage and loan defaults, this depression's immediate cause was the collapse of Ohio Life Insurance and Trust Company, which was deep into railroad stocks. In addition, sales of U.S. farm products declined overseas, although prices of Southern cotton were stable and rising—so the South basically carried the American economy through this brief but severe depression. The government's failure to support business interests led the business community to switch its allegiance to the Republican Party.

Panic of 1873

One of the worst depressions resulted from the too rapid expansion of railroads and the overextension of credit. The immediate cause was the collapse of Jay Cooke & Company, a huge New York bank that was heavily invested in railroads. Within a year, 89 railroads had defaulted on their bonds.

The depression lasted for four years and saw $228 million in business failures and 3 million job losses. Agriculture was affected by falling prices, leading many farmers to default on their loans.

Panic of 1893

Precipitating causes included the bankruptcy of the Philadelphia & Reading Railroad, which sparked a stock market sell-off. The market collapsed, leading to a run on gold reserves. More railroad failures affected industry in general, and some 500 banks and 15,000 businesses failed. Unemployment reached its low point—2.5 to 3 million—in 1894. The government generally responded slowly to the crisis, spawning numerous labor strikes and protests.

Panic of 1907

Overexpansion of industrial production led to wild stock speculation and overextension of credit. When a run on banks began, J. P. Morgan successfully intervened.

This is the first depression in which the government, under President Teddy Roosevelt, really took the reins. Roosevelt ended the gold drain and instituted reforms including:

- Federal incorporation and regulation of all interstate business and the stock market

- Limits on legal injunctions against labor unions and compulsory investigation of all labor disputes

- Implementation of an 8-hour workday for all federal employees

- The imposition of personal income taxes and inheritance taxes

Panic of 1929

The October 1929 stock-market crash resulted from a number of factors and led to the decade-long Great Depression. See What Put the Roar in the Twenties (page 91) and The Real Causes of the Great Depression (page 92).

THE OTHER SIDE OF TRAMPS AND HOBOES

"Riding the rails" has a romantic sound, but it was a rough, dangerous life for the hundreds of thousands of itinerant American men who, for adventure or necessity (especially in hard times), hopped freight cars. These wanderers created a culture that included unique hobo art forms and language.

Whittling was a natural pastime for tramps and hoboes because they were never without their trusty jackknives. Typical carvings included chains carved from a single piece of wood, often in the intricate ball-and-chain style, and buttons whittled from fruit pits.

OUR NATIVE TONGUE

Hobo Lingo

Hoboes created a colorful language of their own. Here's what a Depression-era down-and-outer might have mulled over as he *hit the grit* (walked) on the way to a *jungle* (hobo encampment).

"If I can't find a new pair of *kicks* (shoes) I may have to *gad the hoof* (go barefoot) . . . and how can I make that danged *tombstone* (tooth) stop aching? Maybe I'll come around after I sit by the *smudge* (small campfire) with a hot cup of *mud* (coffee) and some *punk and plaster* (bread and butter).

"I need to start *scraping the pavement* (shaving) to get rid of my face *lace* (whiskers) . . . Lookin' good might make it easier for me to get *strong* (have money) or even *thick* (rich). I'd just as soon not have to *nail a rattler* (hop a train) ever again before I *take the westbound* (die)."

THEY, TOO, MADE THEIR MARK

Edison, Bell, and their famous counterparts tend to overshadow a number of other innovators who deserve a place in history.

JAMES BONSACK: TOBACCO'S REJUVENATOR

Cigarettes had to be rolled by hand until an 18-year-old Virginian invented the cigarette-rolling machine in 1880. Five years before, a Richmond tobacco company had offered a $75,000 prize to anyone who could invent a machine to roll cigarettes. James Bonsack dropped out of school to develop the contraption, and it's unlikely he resumed his studies after he patented the invention that revolutionized the tobacco industry.

JOSEPHINE GARIS COCHRANE: MOTHER OF ALL DISHWASHERS

In 1886 Mrs. Josephine Garis Cochrane, a Victorian socialite, invented the first automatic dishwasher to keep her servants from breaking the family china as they washed it by hand. The hand-operated Garis Cochrane Dishwashing Machine was the hit of the 1893 World's Columbian Exposition in Chicago and subsequently became a staple in many hotels and restaurants.

HERMAN HOLLERITH: OUR FIRST COMPUTER GEEK?

No one is sure when Herman Hollerith, a German-American U.S. Census Bureau engineer, got the idea for a machine that used punched cards to tabulate data (he was not, as myth holds, inspired by a train conductor punching tickets). What's certain is that his invention of the world's first electric machine to read, count, and sort punched cards allowed the 1890 Census data to be tabulated 10 times faster than the 1880 census.

Hollerith founded the Tabulating Machine Company in 1896 and soon was doing a booming business with the New York Central Railroad and clients in England and Russia. In 1911 he agreed to merge with two other companies to form the Computing-Tabulating-Recording Company—an outfit that in 1924 changed its name and went on to become one of the largest corporations in the world: International Business Machines Corporation, or IBM.

CHESTER CARLSON: COPY GUY

In 1938 physicist Chester Carlson invented the dry, or xerographic, method of copying in the back room of his mother-in-law's beauty salon in Queens, New York—giving the world a much neater alternative to the wet mimeograph copiers of the time. Patent royalties on the invention, bought by the Haloid Company (later Xerox) in 1947, made this son of an immigrant Swedish barber a multimillionaire.

Household Names

These born-in-America innovations carry the surnames of their creators.

Colt revolver—Samuel Colt

Dolby noise reduction system— Ray Dolby

Evinrude speedboat motor— Ole Evinrude

Ferris wheel—George Ferris

Franklin stove—Benjamin Franklin

Gatling gun—Richard J. Gatling

Gore-Tex—Wilbert (Bill) Gore

Gillette safety razor—King Gillette

Richter scale—Charles F. Richter

Tupperware—Earl Tupper

SAVIORS NAMED SALK AND SABIN

The trials for the polio vaccine developed by Dr. Jonas Salk with the aid of funds from the March of Dimes (see page 135) came just in time: it was 1952, the year when the worst polio epidemic in American history was reported (57,628 cases). The trials—which took place in the United States, Canada, and Finland and involved 1.8 million children—were designed and directed by Dr. Thomas Francis, Salk's former mentor.

An announcement as anticipated as any in history came on April 12, 1955: The vaccine worked. Schoolchildren began to be vaccinated en masse, and by the end of 1957, new polio cases had dropped almost 90 percent. In 1961 Dr. Albert Sabin introduced an oral vaccine, and by 1980 polio in the United States had been effectively wiped out. In 2005 global cases had dwindled to fewer than 1,300.

FRANK B. COLTON'S PILL

It was 1960 when Searle chemist Frank B. Colton's Enovid-10, the first oral contraceptive, went on sale. Controversial from the beginning, "the pill" ushered in a new age of freedom for women while drawing fire from the Roman Catholic Church and other groups.

Some people held the pill responsible for the sexual revolution, while others believed the new sexual freedom was merely part of the break with the past symbolized by the free speech movement, hippiedom, and feminism. Indeed, Searle's first advertisement for Enovid featured a drawing of the mythical Andromeda throwing off her manacles. The caption, a masterpiece of obfuscation, read in part, "Now [a woman] is permitted normalization, enhancement, or suspension of the cyclic function and procreative potential. This new physiologic control is symbolized in an illustration borrowed from ancient Greek mythology—Andromeda freed from her chains."

Notes on Five of the Most Famous

So what about the inventors you studied in school? Here are five who not only changed life as we know it but whose inventions spawned huge corporations.

Alexander Graham Bell (1847–1922)

- What do you do once you've invented one of the greatest instruments in the world before your thirtieth birthday? If you're Alexander Graham Bell, you spend the rest of your life experimenting.

  Bell's post–telephone innovations included the photophone (which transmitted sound on a beam of light and was the precursor to fiber optics), the metal detector, and the hydrofoil watercraft. Bell also pondered the possibility of heating houses with solar panels.

Thomas Edison (1847–1931)

- America's greatest inventor, whose Edison General Electric Company would become General Electric, wasn't averse to a bit of P. T. Barnum—style showmanship. In 1899 Thomas Edison's new Vitascope projector screened a film of Boer War combat to audiences eager for images from the battles fought between British and Dutch settlers in South Africa.

  However, what viewers thought was the South African landscape was actually rural New Jersey, with locals playing soldier. But who cared if the man who gave us everything from the alkaline battery to the phonograph occasionally gilded the lily?

Elisha Otis (1811–1861)

- Mattress-factory worker Elisha Otis was planning to leave New York for the California gold fields when he devised a "safety hoist" to lift heavy bedding—a platform fitted with a clamp that kept it from falling if a cable snapped. But an unsolicited order for the new device changed his plans. Otis opened a small shop to manufacture the hoists, but after a year in business his sales fell short of the $12 million he had projected—way short, by $11,910,000.

  Undaunted, Otis developed a passenger safety elevator, the first of which (complete with chandeliers) was installed at E. V. Haughwaut & Company, importer of fine French china, in lower New York in 1857. Seven decades later, it was Otis's elevator that would make skyscrapers a practical reality.

Isaac Singer (1811–1875)

- In his youth, Isaac Singer became an actor—the first of several unsuccessful ventures. But when the born tinkerer set out to make Elias Howe's sewing machine more user-friendly, things changed. I. M. Singer & Company took off and became one of the world's first multinational companies.

  Singer was larger than life, and not just because he stood 6' 4" tall. He had five wives and 23 children, and his common-law wife Mary Ann Sponsler later had him arrested for bigamy. And if that weren't enough, one of Singer's grandchildren was born out of wedlock to his son Paris and the modern dance sensation Isadora Duncan.

George Westinghouse (1846–1914)

- George Westinghouse's first triumph was the invention of the air brake for trains (an achievement that his *New York Times* obituary writer claimed "saved more lives than centuries of warfare have destroyed"). He later developed a system for delivering electricity to homes. In the contest between two fathers of invention that was called the War of the Currents (1880s and '90s), Westinghouse's alternating current prevailed over Edison's direct current, which was limited in both reach and voltage flexibility.

DIDN'T HAPPEN!

Goodyear Founded Goodyear Tire & Rubber

After five years of failed experimentation with substances that would keep rubber from melting in heat and hardening in cold weather, Charles Goodyear struck gold in 1839—sulfur, with properties that would make rubber weatherproof.

A poor businessman, the then 39-year-old made some bad deals and lost money fighting 32 cases against patent pirates at home and abroad. When Goodyear died in 1860, he was $200,000 in debt. But his name lived on when, in 1898, Akron native Frank A. Seiberling began to manufacture tires and named his company Goodyear Tire & Rubber in honor of the man who made rubber usable and useful.

THE THIRD WAVE

THE THIRD INDUSTRIAL REVOLUTION WAS A TIDAL WAVE THAT
STARTED WITH THE U.S. SPACE PROGRAM AND SWEPT ON TO THE
IT REVOLUTION.

ROCKET MAN

During his early experimentation with liquid-fueled rockets, Robert
H. Goddard—a physics professor at Clark University in Worcester,
Massachusetts—suffered the slings and arrows of the skeptics. It
became worse when he dared to speculate in a published paper that
rockets might reach the Moon someday. A January 13, 1920, editorial
in the *New York Times* accused him of lacking even "the knowledge
ladled out daily in high schools."

The ridicule didn't abate after Goddard succeeded in launching
a series of small rockets in local farm fields between 1926 and 1929.
Retreating to New Mexico, he launched bigger rockets to greater
heights, but these, too, were ignored—though Goddard did give
advice to the German scientists who occasionally consulted him.

It was the Germans who found a practical application for Goddard's rocket, when building the V-2 missiles that bombed London
in World War II. After Goddard's death in 1945, American physicists
collaborated with German-born physicist Wernher von Braun to convert the V-2 into the Redstone, the rocket that put the first Americans
in space. Nevertheless, it took the *New York Times* until 1969 to
retract its criticism of the man who had become known as the father
of modern rocketry. (See also The Moon Rocks! Or Not, page 74.)

THE *REALLY* INTERNATIONAL SPACE STATION

The diverse crew isn't the only worldly aspect of the International Space Station (ISS). Several of its modules were manufactured outside of the United States, including these:

- The Russian Zarya and Zveda modules, with living quarters and life support equipment

- The Canadian Canadarm2, a new-generation robot that serves as the ISS's space crane

- The Japanese Kibu experiment module, where four astronauts can work on experiments at the same time

- The Italian Node 3 connecting module, housing life support equipment for the crew of six

A COMPUTER THE SIZE OF A HOUSE

In February 1946 J. Presler Eckert and John Mauchly, engineers at the University of Pennsylvania, introduced ENIAC (Electrical Numerical Integrator And Calculator), the first computer to use electrical pulses. It occupied 1,800 feet of floor space and used 7,468 vacuum tubes and 180,000 watts of electrical power. The Ballistics Research Laboratory, the branch of the U.S. military responsible for calculating artillery-firing data, sponsored Eckert and Mauchly's research.

The engineers soon formed a corporation that was bought by Remington Rand in 1950. Rand completed the pair's work on the UNIVAC (UNIVersal Automatic Computer) and delivered this first commercial computer to the U.S. Census Bureau in March 1951.

Successive generations of computers shrank as vacuum tubes became obsolete and were replaced by transistors (late 1950s), integrated circuits (mid-1960s), and microprocessors (1971), the last with thousands of integrated circuits in a single silicon chip. Computers, once enormous, could now be no bigger than a cigarette lighter.

BILL AND PAUL'S EXCELLENT ADVENTURE

It's probably far-fetched to think that Bill Gates wouldn't be Bill Gates if his private school hadn't installed an ASR-33 Teletype machine in 1968. But there's no doubt that experimenting with a mechanism that could "talk" to an actual computer—a PDP-10 (Program Data Processor) in downtown Seattle—set him on the road. A teacher at the Lakeside School in Seattle took Bill, an eighth-grade math whiz, and his classmates to see how the Teletype worked and allowed Bill to type in a few commands—whereupon the Teletype printed out its response!

The school began to let students hang out in the Teletype room, and Bill jumped at the chance to write programs of the tic-tac-toe ilk. Tenth-grader Paul Allen also frequented the Teleptype room, and the pair forged a friendship rooted in their belief that the possibilities for computer technology were unlimited. Seven years later they made good on their promise when they founded Microsoft—and the rest, as they say, is history.

Wired in the White House

FDR's fireside chats allowed him to forge a bond with the public. JFK was forever linked with TV after he came off better than Nixon in history's first televised debate; next to Nixon's camera-enhanced five o'clock shadow, Kennedy appeared especially young and vibrant.

In 2009 Barack Obama broke new ground by becoming the first wired president, so reliant on 21st century technology he was loath to give up his BlackBerry. Yet necessity dictated that his beloved device be used only for communicating with family and friends, while a super–encrypted smartphone—the particulars of which are kept secret—would serve for government business. The brief brouhaha serves as a reminder that, figuratively speaking, today's presidents most certainly "aren't in Kansas anymore."

Success sans Degrees

There's a long-standing notion that a college degree is the only route to a good job, but some gazillionaires of the last 2 years have proved otherwise. None of these dozen men ever graduated from college:

Paul Allen	Bill Gates
John Jacob Astor	J. Paul Getty
Andrew Carnegie	William Randolph Hearst
George Eastman	Steve Jobs
Thomas Edison	John D. Rockefeller Sr.
Henry Ford	Cornelius Vanderbilt

ENTER HTTP://WWW

The World Wide Web may have been developed by Englishman Tim Berners-Lee and Belgian Robert Cailliau, but when it made its August 1991 debut on the Internet—the information superhighway on which the IT Revolution speeds—the lives of people everywhere changed forever. Even in the 1980s we couldn't have imagined instant communication with friends, business associates, and even potential spouses (or lovers) in another corner of the globe—often while looking them in the face! Nor could we have fathomed the ease with which we can access information with a click of the mouse, however iffy some of that info may be.

Indeed, the world is our oyster. Web users number more than a billion, so each of us could theoretically communicate with every sixth person on the planet if, in the words of the poet Andrew Marvell, "had we world enough, and time."

Buildings to Burials

Our Daily Lives

Where we live tells a lot about how we live. In the great scheme of history, the United States remains a young country where new ideas sprout and grow like weeds. We see wacky fads come, and we watch thankfully as most of them go. But some things have permanence and link us to our past. Almanacs are still sold, children still wave flags on the Fourth of July, brides still wear white, we all still love a juicy celebrity scandal. And our American dreams still begin with our families and our homes.

HOME AND HEARTH

To make America their home, new arrivals had to build houses and neighborhoods. Their earliest shelters were barely habitable, but the migrants learned to make do and move forward.

DESPERATELY SEEKING COMPANY

It's told that during his years as a Virginia farmer, George Washington would become so starved for lively conversation that he'd stand at the Mount Vernon gate and invite anyone who happened by to dinner. Although Southerners made the most of every chance to socialize, they lacked the compulsory church services and town meetings that regularly brought New Englanders together.

Good roads, railroads, and mail service were slow to develop, and even into the 20th century, many Southerners never traveled more than a few miles beyond their place of birth. The passing stranger or itinerant salesman was their only contact with the outside world. So when Southerners said, "Y'all come back," they meant it.

LITTLE HOUSES ON THE FRONTIER

Settlers on the Western frontier often lived in underground dugouts before moving into a sod house, or soddy. They may sound flimsy, but soddies were more stable and better insulated than the drafty, windowless wood huts built by the New England colonists, although the bricks of dried sod tended to crumble and attracted insects, small critters, and snakes.

Poor Richard's Almanac Prank

The two books found in most colonial homes were the family Bible and an almanac. The earliest American almanacs were straightforward listings of seasonal and navigation data. As competition increased, almanac printers attracted buyers by adding stories, moral sayings, bawdy jokes, horoscopes, poems, and predictions. One dire prediction ignited a comic feud.

In his 1733 edition of *Poor Richard's Almanac,* Benjamin Franklin, writing as Richard Saunders, predicted that rival printer Titan Leeds would die "on Oct. 17.1733.3 ho. 29 m. P.M." Leeds didn't die, wasn't amused, and loudly protested. Franklin responded that indeed Leeds was dead and an imposter had taken his place. The back and forth continued until Leeds really died in 1738.

Franklin cribbed his prank from an infamous almanac feud perpetrated by Jonathan Swift in 1708. Franklin also lifted most of Poor Richard's sayings from British sources, a practice neither illegal nor uncommon in the days before copyright laws.

Scandinavians arriving in the middle colonies in the 1600s brought another option—the log cabin—which became the standard in frontier areas where trees were plentiful. Snug and watertight (sod house roofs frequently collapsed in heavy rains), log houses were easy to build and enlarge. An eyewitness account of building a log dwelling is found in *Little House on the Prairie* by Laura Ingalls Wilder, who was born in a log cabin in Wisconsin in 1867.

SPITS, PINCHES, DIPS

Before manufactured cigarettes, tobacco was mostly chewed, which necessitated spitting, and men weren't particular about where they spat. Foreign visitors sent home nauseating reports of American floors and walkways, including the marbled halls of Congress, slimy with tobacco residue and fine carpets stained brown. A stroll left skirts and trouser cuffs caked with the stuff. Juries spat tobacco during trials, and even clergymen had to be warned not to spit in church.

Well-bred women rarely chewed, but many, including Dolley Madison, enjoyed sniffing pinches of snuff. Dipping—rubbing snuff on the upper front teeth and gum—was also popular, although it ruined many a pretty smile. Smokers favored long-stemmed pipes or Caribbean cigars.

THE BOARDING HOUSE REACH

An estimated 70 percent of 19th-century Americans lived in boarding houses at some time in their lives. Running a boarding house was traditionally the province of poor widows, but the population shift from farms to factories, particularly among young, single people, created a need that all the widows in the country couldn't meet. So organizations including the YMCA and YWCA began operating urban boarding facilities. In Chicago, Hull House founder Jane Addams and union activist Mary Kenney set up the Jane Club, a cooperative house for single working women.

The term *boarding house* goes back to colonial days, when the family dining table was just two or three rough wood boards laid across sawhorses. Room and board houses—which offered a bedroom plus meals—became simply boarding houses, and their paying occupants, boarders.

NEW YORKERS ON THE MOVE

In 19th and early 20th century New York City, May Day was a moving experience. Rental contracts were traditionally renewed on the first of May, so that was the day people changed their addresses. On April 30, 1859, *Harper's Weekly* magazine published a comic engraving of chaos on a New York street corner with this observation: "Every one is moving; no one has a house; every one is miserable except the licensed cartmen [movers], who are in their seventh heaven . . . and the boys, who are blissful at the prospect of excitement." Moving day originated with the Dutch settlers, and it's estimated that as many as a third of all Manhattanites changed residence annually—most on May Day.

THOSE INCONVENIENT CONVENIENCES

Household improvements—from dust-catching velvet drapes and wool rugs to soot-spewing gas lights, wood-burning stoves, and central heating—usually made the middle-class housewife's work harder and increased the time she spent cleaning. Their colonial grandmothers had paid little attention to cleanliness, but Victorian women were encouraged to make a fetish of it. Although some new conveniences—Melville Bissell's carpet sweeper, linoleum flooring, flush toilets—were helpful, most didn't fulfill their promises. Sixty-five years elapsed between the introduction of wringer clothes washers in 1805 and the production of a design that wasn't backbreaking.

Middle-class families also crammed their houses with overstuffed furniture and decorative bric-a-brac that required endless dusting. So when Americans saw the spare lines and simple décor of a Japanese house exhibited at the 1876 Philadelphia Centennial Exposition, many overworked homemakers jumped at this excuse to go home and de-clutter.

WHARTON WAXES WISE ON HOME DÉCOR

New York socialite Edith Wharton, one of America's greatest novelists, also had a strong affinity for home design and landscaping. Her first book, *The Decoration of Houses* (1897), co-written with Ogden Codman Jr., is considered the founding document of professional interior design.

Wharton was raised amid wealth and privilege in New York City and Newport, Rhode Island. When her father ran into money problems, the family decamped to Europe until things improved.

Exposed to the best of both continents, Edith developed the critical eye for physical details that she shared with Codman, an MIT-trained architect. They championed simplicity, gently mocked Gilded Age excesses, and proposed a radical idea—collaboration between architects and designers in the creation of homes.

WELCOME HOME, SOLDIERS

Soldiers returning from France in 1919 had received only a small check, a ticket home, and a pat on the back. Determined to do better by War World II vets, Congress, the Roosevelt administration, and veterans' organizations developed the Servicemen's Readjustment Act of 1944—the G.I. Bill—a $14 billion benefits package that included government-backed home, farm, and business loans.

Between 1944 and 1956, the Veterans Administration guaranteed close to 2.4 million low-interest home loans, sparking a construction boom that buoyed the economy. In less than 20 years, the government recovered the taxpayers' entire investment in the G.I.s.

"We Ordered It from Sears"

Between 1908 and 1940, the easiest way for families to get their dream house was by mail order. Sears offered almost 450 house styles. These "Modern Homes" were not just architectural plans but entire houses—from precut timber framing to baseboards and stained glass windows—shipped by rail and delivered to the site. In an impressive example of the scope of industrialization and standardization, Sears mass-produced houses that could be fit together by local builders in less time and at lower cost than custom construction. More than 70,000 Sears houses were sold, and many still look like a million bucks.

While the house plans were diverse and attractive, they weren't architecturally daring. But they did include technological advances (balloon framing, asphalt shingles, drywall, central heat systems, electrical wiring, indoor bathrooms) that enabled ordinary Americans to enjoy the good life at home.

MARRYING AND BREAKING UP

COLONIAL AMERICANS COURTED QUICKLY, MARRIED YOUNG,
AND STAYED HITCHED UNTIL DEATH DID THEM PART.
THAT BEGAN TO CHANGE IN THE 1800S, THANKS IN
PART TO SOME HIGH-PROFILE SCANDALS.

MARRIED IN THEIR BIRTHDAY SUITS (ALMOST)

When a colonial widow remarried, there was a tradition that all her
and her deceased husband's debts would be cancelled if she wore
nothing more than a thin shift for her next wedding. In 1893, folk-
lorist Alice Earle recounted a number of these "smock marriages."
There was the nearly nude bride who stayed in a closet for her wedding service; another who crouched in a curtained chimney recess;
and still another who stood on the top of a tall ladder in the dead of
night to take her vows, then dressed before descending. The "most
curious" of all, Earle wrote, was a 1784 smock wedding on a hanging gallows by which the publicly exposed bride won a last-minute
reprieve for her new husband.

LICENSED TO WED

The customary Anglican "banns" announcing an upcoming marriage didn't translate well to the rural Southern colonies. Most
Southern settlers were Anglican, but because of the long distances
between farm and town, they rarely attended church services. Yet
weddings were important community celebrations, and everyone had
to be invited. Since "posting the banns" from the pulpit was point-
less, Virginians innovated the marriage license, filed with the county

All in Good Fun

"Riding for the ribbon" was a Scotch-Irish wedding custom—a group of riders or a lone horseman made a wild dash to the bride's home to claim a bottle of whiskey tied with a ribbon. Celebratory gunfire was common in the Southern and Middle colonies and later in the West, and dangerous in light of the quantities of alcohol consumed. Other pranks included kidnapping the bride or groom and demanding a liquid ransom, felling large trees to block the newlyweds' departure, and parading a new bride around town in a wheelbarrow.

The shivaree, from the French *charivari,* was a rowdy post-nuptial ritual popular in the South and West in the 19th and early 20th centuries. Friends mock-serenaded the bridal couple immediately or a few days after the ceremony. Banging pots, ringing bells, and singing at full volume, they made a commotion until the newlyweds bought their silence with food and drink. Today's custom of tying cans or shoes to a couple's car originated with the shivaree.

clerk. Farmers routinely traveled to their county seats to do business and get the latest news; they could easily learn about impending marriages by checking the official licenses at the courthouse.

Use of marriage licenses spread northward and also inspired early "marriage mills." Less than scrupulous justices of the peace would keep a stock of blank license forms, ready to be filled out by eloping couples—for a fee.

EXTRA! EXTRA! WEDDING JUMPS THE SHARK!

High society one-upmanship peaked with the November 1895 wedding of Consuelo Vanderbilt, daughter of William Kissam Vanderbilt, to Charles Richard John Spencer-Churchill, the impoverished ninth Duke of Marlborough. As a dowry, Vanderbilt gave his future son-in-law $2.5 million in railroad stock. Consuelo's controlling mother, Alva, pulled out all the stops. A few highlights from the extensive newspaper coverage of the event follow.

Site: The very large Saint Thomas's Protestant Episcopal Church, New York City

Wedding invitations sent: 4,000

Music: A 50-piece symphony orchestra and a 60-voice choir

Officiants: Total of two bishops, one reverend, and three reverends in reserve

Bride's gown: Cream satin heavily trimmed with Brussels lace, chiffon, and orange blossoms; a 15-foot-long satin train embroidered with seed pearls

Flowers: Laurel garlands draped from the church's 95-foot dome, six floral Gothic arches, walls of white roses and chrysanthemums, and enough palm trees and cut flowers to obscure the church's interior

Uninvited guests: Thousands of gawkers who ignored the police and risked being crushed under the carriages of the rich and famous

The New York Times gushed that the wedding "was, without exception, the most magnificent ever celebrated in this country." Alva later admitted she had forced her daughter into a loveless marriage.

AMERICA'S FIRST CELEBRITY BREAKUP

Among the first American women to make a Cinderella marriage was Elizabeth "Betsy" Patterson of Baltimore, the pretty and fashionable daughter of a wealthy Irish immigrant. In 1803, Betsy, age 17, met a visiting Frenchman, Jerome Bonaparte, the 19-year-old brother of Napoleon, and the couple soon wed. On learning of the marriage, Napoleon ordered it annulled. Thinking the emperor could be dissuaded, Jerome and Betsy, now pregnant, sailed for France, but Betsy was denied entry into continental Europe. She finally found haven in England, where her son was born. Jerome eventually gave in to his brother's demands and married a German princess to further Napoleon's political ambitions.

Returning to the United States, Betsy was legally divorced by an act of the Maryland legislature in 1815, although she continued to claim the Bonaparte name and her son's right to inherit. Divorce was scandalous at the time, yet most Americans took Betsy's side. Still, she never remarried and died, rich and embittered, at the age of 94.

Divorce Would Have Been Easier

When the parties are well known and the outcome is murder, a sordid love story becomes a public sensation. Among the titillating cases from the country's past:

1857 Congressman Daniel Sickles shot and killed Philip Barton Key on the sidewalk opposite the White House. The son of Francis Scott Key and nephew of Supreme Court Chief Justice Roger Taney, Key was a respected Washington district attorney and the lover of Sickles's wife, Teresa. A notorious philanderer, Sickles claimed temporary insanity and was acquitted—the first successful insanity defense in American legal history.

1869 Abby McFarland divorced her abusive husband, Daniel, and was set to wed popular *New York Tribune* editor Albert Richardson, until Daniel showed up at Richardson's office and shot him. Daniel McFarland said he was defending his family and was acquitted. Mrs. McFarland had married Richardson in a deathbed ceremony performed by Henry Ward Beecher. Three years later, Beecher was entangled in his own adultery scandal; no one died, but the pious pastor's reputation never recovered.

1883 Attorney and politician Nicholas Dukes of Uniontown, Pennsylvania, falsely accused his fiancée, Lizzie Nutt, of being intimate with other men. In a quarrel with her father, Dukes killed the older gentleman but claimed self-defense and was acquitted. Disbarred and forced to resign from the Pennsylvania legislature, he was later shot down by Lizzie's brother, who pled insanity and was acquitted.

RAISING FAMILIES

EARLY AMERICAN FAMILIES FUNCTIONED LIKE SMALL INDUSTRIES;
EVERYONE WORKED TOGETHER. BUT THE RISE OF THE MIDDLE
CLASS BROUGHT A SEPARATION OF DOMESTIC RESPONSIBILITIES.

DOMESTIC GODDESSES

As Americans became more urbanized, the nature of middle-class
family life changed. Duties that once overlapped were separated.
Husbands became the breadwinners and decision makers. Children
were transformed into little darlings to be pampered and petted. And
wives were sentimentalized as fragile, intellectually limited angels yet
were expected to create peaceful sanctuaries for their hardworking
men and raise perfect children. Household servants and children's
nannies, symbols of middle-class affluence, deprived many housewives of actual work.

Led by *Godey's Lady's Book,* the women's magazine industry
overflowed with advice for the new class of bored, unhappy domestic
goddesses. Sarah Josepha Hale, the widowed mother of five who edited
Godey's for 40 years (from 1837 to 1877), strongly supported female
education but opposed suffrage and much else that might get wives
out of the house. As modern scholars have noted, it's strange that
Hale, the model of a high-achieving single working mom, should have
been so dead set on keeping others of her gender stuck at home.

WOMEN BY SPECIAL DELIVERY

Opening the West was man's business. Men went first; women
and children followed after some semblance of civilized living

was achieved. From logging camps to boom towns, the shortage of marriageable women (the kind a fellow would introduce to his mother) was so severe that men filled East Coast newspapers with personal ads offering themselves as husbands. The heyday of so-called "mail-order brides" followed the Civil War and lasted into the 20th century.

Women often traveled in organized groups. The "Mercer Girls" of the mid-1860s was one such group. Asa Mercer, president of the University of Washington, traveled east to recruit female teachers for Seattle's schools. Most women couldn't afford the $250 cost of the long sea journey, but Mercer assembled nearly a dozen, ranging in age from 15 to 35. His second trip east yielded almost three dozen more. The women taught school; they also married and raised families. Although Mercer fell far short of his recruitment goal of 700, he won a prize—his wife, Anne.

HEADING WEST: "ORPHAN TRAINS"

Between 1853 and 1929, an estimated 100,000 orphaned or abandoned children were relocated from New York primarily to the Midwest and West. This migration was the project of Charles Loring Brace, a minister, social worker, and head of the New York Children's Aid Society. Brace was determined to rescue homeless children of all ages, from infants to teenagers, from orphanages and other forbidding public institutions.

Transported by "orphan trains," the children were placed with people willing to raise them as their own. No money was exchanged. Society inspectors visited the families and could remove any child who was mistreated. Amazingly for such a large undertaking, most of the children found good homes and grew up to be solid citizens, including at least one governor and several congressmen.

The Society had its critics, but what eventually ended the project was improved social services for the poor, the development of our foster care system, and the new doctrine that families should be kept intact whenever possible.

IMAGES OF TENEMENT LIFE

In the Gilded Age, wealthy and middle-class city dwellers avoided poor neighborhoods, but the 1890 publication of New York journalist Jacob Riis's *How the Other Half Lives* opened their eyes. A Danish immigrant, Riis worked as a police reporter for the *New York Tribune* and the Associated Press and knew well the "foul alleys and fouler tenements" of the city. As a writer and self-taught photographer, Riis became an advocate. His stark photos exposing the realities of life for poor families and the callousness of the vast majority of landlords stirred the city's conscience and hastened reforms. Theodore Roosevelt called Riis "the most useful citizen of New York."

Riis's use of photography gave a new weapon to social reformers, inspiring the later work of Lewis Hine, who documented child labor, and of Dorothea Lange, Margaret Bourke-White, and Walker Evans, who recorded the poor and homeless during the Great Depression.

LEARNING WITH DICK AND JANE

Most American schoolchildren learned to read from textbooks—mainly *The New England Primer* and *McGuffey's Reader*—that mixed the ABCs with heavy doses of religious moralizing. Then Dick and Jane stories were introduced into elementary schools in the 1930s. These charmingly illustrated stories and books took another tack: early phonetic reading in the context of white middle-class values. Attempts to update the books' lily-white, suburban fantasy (an African American family moved into the neighborhood in the mid-1960s) never quite worked, and the series was retired in 1970—gone but not forgotten by the estimated 85 million Americans who grew up with Dick and Jane.

THE MANY, MANY, MANY BOOMERS

The Baby Boom is not a generation. It was a demographic anomaly that began in the United States with a relatively small and not unexpected rise in birth rates that began in 1946 and ended in 1964, when the birth rate returned to its 1946 level. (The annual birth rate is the percentage of live births per 1,000 people.) During the Boom, almost 79 million American babies were born.

Demographers and marketers separate the Boom into two waves—boomers born before the end of the Korean War and boomers born after—because people born on either side of the divide had very different upbringings, experiences, aspirations, and opportunities. Compare, for example, Presidents Bill Clinton and George W. Bush, born in the first year of the Boom, and President Barack Obama, born in 1961, near the end of the second wave of boomers.

Unlike subsequent population clusters (Slackers, Gen-Xers, Millennials), the Boomers got their collective name from government statisticians.

The Pastor's Big Fibs

Mason Locke Weems, born in Maryland in 1759, was an Anglican minister who supplemented his income by peddling books from the back of a wagon. Both jovial and temperamental, Pastor Weems loved money and had a sharp instinct for the literary tastes of his countrymen. These characteristics came together in his great idea—to write a stirring patriotic biography of the nation's hero.

A History of the Life and Death, Virtues and Exploits, of General George Washington was published in 1800, the year after the first president's death. Full of uplifting anecdotes and moral messages, the book was so beloved that publication continued until 1927 (at least 83 editions are known). But much of the lively *History* was fiction—including the famous accounts of young George's admission that he chopped down his father's cherry tree and General George's pious prayer in the snow at Valley Forge. Whether Pastor Weems intentionally fibbed or was swept away by poetic license is still debatable.

THE FOOD ON OUR TABLES

THE IDEA THAT FOOD COULD BE PLEASURABLE WAS A HARD SELL
IN EARLY AMERICA. THEN NEW TECHNOLOGIES AND THE
INTRODUCTION OF VARIETY IN THE DAILY DIET CHANGED TASTES.

DON'T DRINK THE WATER!

The early colonists didn't like water, didn't trust it, and only drank
it when nothing else was available. This early avoidance may have
had some basis in their urban backgrounds; water in English and
European cites was often dirty and polluted, and some people were
beginning to connect bad water to disease outbreaks. Whatever the
reason, the colonists favored milk from goats and cows, although milk
was problematic in the South because of rapid spoilage. Southerners
probably adapted to water drinking earlier than New Englanders, who
preferred hard cider as a thirst quencher even for children, but the
general prejudice against water persisted for several generations.

HEALTH NUTS

In the late 1820s, Americans went health crazy. It was the beginning
of a century that would see huge leaps forward in medical and biological science. But many food fads were based on religious scripture and
biological guesswork. The new fascination with healthy diets brought
out scores of cranks, quacks, and charlatans along with well-meaning
but wrong-headed food fanatics including Sylvester Graham, John
Harvey Kellogg, and Charles William Post.

    Sylvester Graham (1794–1851), a Presbyterian minister known
      for his eloquence and arrogance, began by crusading against

alcohol but expanded his field to encompass food and sexual activity. Drawing on Biblical texts, Graham determined that strict vegetarianism would cure all bodily evils, especially alcoholism, lust, and masturbation. He and his followers, known as Grahamites, agitated against commercially baked white bread and promoted dark bread made from coarsely ground wheat dubbed "Graham flour" (the main ingredient in modern Graham crackers). His meatless, spiceless, bread-heavy, and water-only diet was so tasteless that Ralph Waldo Emerson called him "the philosopher of sawdust pudding."

John Harvey Kellogg (1852–1943), physician and Seventh Day Adventist, picked up on Graham's themes but was taken more seriously because of his medical expertise. A less rigid vegetarian than Graham, Kellogg's obsession was the intestinal tract and bowel, and yogurt enemas were administered daily to the upper-class patrons at his Battle Creek, Michigan, health sanitarium, owned by the Adventists. (If yogurt didn't clean up the patient, Dr. Kellogg would surgically remove a section of the intestine.)

The doctor and his brother Will invented and manufactured cornflakes and other breakfast foods but parted ways when Will, who added sugar to the flakes, left to start the Kellogg company in 1906. Egocentric and quarrelsome, Dr. Kellogg also promoted sexual abstinence, and over more than 40 years, he never consummated his own marriage—a deprivation said to be an experiment to prove it could be done.

Charles William Post (1854–1914) opened a rival health center focused on mind-body cures. The clinic failed, but his Postum Cereal Company, founded in 1895, made him a multimillionaire. Post manufactured cereal-based products including Grape-Nuts, Elijah's Manna (later rechristened Post Toasties), and Postum, a coffee substitute made with wheat bran and molasses. His legendary advertising campaigns appealed to health-conscious Americans through grossly exaggerated claims.

In March 1914, Post underwent successful surgery for acute appendicitis, but possibly depressed by pain, he committed suicide two months later, leaving his only child, Marjorie, and her husband, stockbroker E. F. Hutton, to run the Post empire.

Where Everyone Knew Your Name

Before Swiss brothers Peter and John Delmonico opened their first restaurant in Manhattan in 1827, eating out for pleasure was an alien concept to Americans. The brothers offered something extraordinary—printed menus, excellent French cuisine, solicitous service from skilled waiters, tasteful décor, and soft music—in other words, formal dining, a million miles away from the tavern and street vendor meals Americans were accustomed to.

Within a generation, more than 5,000 restaurants were up and running in New York, and the trend had spread to urban centers nationwide. Although Delmonico's, or "Del's," became a haven for social snobs, it operated democratically; women were welcomed, and no one who could pay was turned away. The restaurant thrived for nearly a century, until Prohibition forced it to close in 1923.

HOW THE UPPER CRUST DINED

Lavish dinner parties hosted by the Gilded Age rich rivaled the feasts of ancient Rome, but few were as creative as the 1903 banquet hosted by Cornelius Kingsley Garrison Billings for 36 friends at New York's Sherry's restaurant. One of Sherry's ballrooms was decorated as a park, complete with a sod carpet, and 36 horses were lifted in. The men dined on horseback—eating from trays mounted on their saddles and sipping champagne through rubber straws from bottles in their saddlebags.

Billings, a Chicago utilities magnate and founding chairman of Union Carbide, was celebrating the opening of the 33-horse, 22-carriage stable at his Upper Manhattan mansion. Reports of his extravagance fascinated and angered the public and speeded the end of the era's gold-plated excesses.

THOSE HEAVENLY "HARVEY GIRLS"

English-born Fred Harvey, sensing that leisure travel via railroad was the coming thing, contracted with the Atchison Topeka Santa Fe rail company to build restaurants along the lines. His first Harvey House opened in Topeka, Kansas, in 1876 staffed with young men.

By 1883 Harvey was fed up with irresponsible and often loutish male servers. He decided to recruit and hire only young, single women "of good character, attractive and intelligent." They became known as "Harvey Girls" and were a welcome sight to hungry, weary rail passengers throughout the Southwest. Fred Harvey's employment experiment—plus excellent food and clean, attractive surroundings—was wildly successful, and the Harvey empire, including hotels and railway dining cars, continued to grow when it passed to his son and son-in-law after the founder's death in 1901.

57 WAYS TO DO GOOD IN BUSINESS

Henry John Heinz's German-Lutheran parents hoped he'd become a minister, but the boy's business acumen surfaced at age 8, when he began selling produce from his mother's Pittsburgh garden. After his first grown-up business failed in 1877, Heinz, his brother, and a cousin launched the firm that became the H. J. Heinz Company. Heinz soon proved as adept at marketing as manufacturing; he created the slogan "57 Varieties" and personally designed the company's distinctive condiment bottles and labels. His factories were models of cleanliness, efficiency, and positive labor relations. The radical International Brotherhood of Electrical Workers called his operations "a utopia for working men." Unlike other food processors, Heinz demanded the highest standards of food quality and hygiene and bucked the rest of his industry to fight for the 1906 Pure Food and Drug Act, the legal foundation for federal inspection and regulation.

VICTORY GARDENS: IF YOU WANT IT, GROW IT

The fiction has patriotic citizens during World War II gallantly forgoing sugar, coffee, meat, canned fish, cheese, butter, and eggs to support the boys fighting overseas. But in fact, most Americans hated wartime food rationing. The miracle is that so many complied with the government's complicated system.

Victory gardening eased the pain. Urged to supplement their diets with homegrown produce, people tilled backyards, parks, vacant lots, and even hauled dirt to city rooftops. Mrs. Roosevelt had part of the White House lawn converted to a vegetable garden. In a canning frenzy, Americans purchased 315,000 pressure cookers in 1943, almost five times the number bought the previous year. Before rationing was lifted, an estimated 20 million victory gardens yielded some 9 to 10 million tons of fresh produce, equal to all commercial vegetable production in the same years.

THE FIZZIEST PLACE IN TOWN

For more than a century, the drugstore soda fountain was *the* gathering place. Considered a health tonic since the late 1700s, carbonated water was first sold in a Philadelphia pharmacy in 1825. Druggists and other innovators began adding flavorings and bottling the fizzy stuff. (And yes, early soda drinks often contained cocaine, added for "pep.") The acknowledged "Soda Fountain King" was John Matthews

(1808–1870), an English immigrant and the driving force behind the rapid growth of soda sales. Matthews is buried in Brooklyn under an ornate marble sculpture of a soda fountain.

Drugstore fountains, many offering luncheonette meals, flourished until World War II, when soda jerks (the white-coated young men who dispensed drinks) were drafted and sugar was rationed. Revived after the war, soda fountains faced heavy competition from fast-food chains and soft-drink bottlers. Most vanished in the 1960s. Their ghosts linger in today's self-serve drink dispensers, but gone is the romance of flirting with your best girl or guy over "one soda, two straws."

DIDN'T HAPPEN!

The Chef Was a Spy

America's "French Chef," Julia Child, changed the way we cook by opening our eyes, noses, and taste buds to the possibilities of fresh ingredients cooked well in the average home kitchen. But do news accounts of classified CIA documents released in 2008 really confirm the old story of her "secret career" as a World War II spy?

Rejected for the women's army and naval corps because she was too tall, Julia Carolyn McWilliams of California worked for the Office of Strategic Services (OSS, the forerunner of the CIA) in Washington—as a typist and clerical assistant. She became an administrative assistant for the OSS's Emergency Sea Rescue Equipment section ("the only time I really got out of the files," she later recalled), then went to Ceylon (Sri Lanka) in 1944 as Chief of the OSS Registry, a position requiring top security clearance. Julia worked with spies, but was the French Chef also an American Mata Hari? In a word, *non*.

THE CLOTHES ON OUR BACKS

THE EARLY COLONISTS DIDN'T CARE HOW THEY LOOKED, BUT AS SOON AS AMERICANS STARTED MAKING MONEY, THEY EXPANDED THEIR WARDROBES, AND FASHION BECAME HIGHLY FASHIONABLE.

PERIWIGS AND PONYTAILS

Colonial men kept their hair short, but around 1700, younger men let it grow to their collars, worrying parents, clergy, and the established authorities. Soon after, rebellious youths with money were shaving their heads and donning "periwigs," a fashion passed from the French to the English and the colonies.

Any man in a wig was assumed to be a gentleman. Men of the "middling" class—farmers, craftsmen, ordinary soldiers—didn't take to wigs but did let their hair grow, tying it back in a "queue," or pony-tail. Wigs and tails remained fashionable until short hair made a comeback in the early 1800s.

THE SKINNY ON MEN'S OUTFITS

Around 1800, men began giving up short pants for long, slimly cut trousers worn with linen shirts and trim waist-length jackets with tails. Lace-up leather shoes were introduced. The tri-cornered hat of the Revolutionary period gave way to taller, narrow-brim styles that became stovepipes by President Lincoln's day. Although men's styles varied from time to time, well-dressed males essentially spent the 19th century creating the classic American business suit of trousers, short jacket, and plain shirt.

LITTLE LORD FAUNTLEROY

Just when it seemed boys under age 12 might be freed of their cursed knickers, Frances Hodgson Burnett decided to write *Little Lord Fauntleroy* (1886)—the *Harry Potter* of its day. To aid the costume designer for the play produced from her best-selling novel, Mrs. Burnett supplied a photograph of her younger son, Vivian, dressed in velvet knee pants and a tailed jacket trimmed with a lace collar and cuffs. Long sausage curls and a broad feathered hat were added, and the Little Lord Fauntleroy look, beloved by mothers everywhere, was born.

Vivian Burnett had worn the foppish outfit to perform in a charity concert, and for the rest of his life was acutely embarrassed by his accidental role in starting the Fauntleroy fashion fad—although probably not as embarrassed as the boys forced to wear such attire in public.

DIDN'T HAPPEN!

Mrs. Bloomer's Bloomers

The clothing and underclothing worn by 19th-century women was little short of torture. Tight, boned corsets literally took their breath away. Heavy, billowing skirts and petticoats made exercise impossible. Doctors became alarmed at the number of illnesses, from unexplained fainting to spinal deformities, they suspected were related to restrictive clothing. Mid-century suffragists, including Amelia Jenks Bloomer, publisher of the country's first newspaper for women, demanded dress reform.

The reformers wore and promoted the "bifurcated skirt"—a knee-length dress worn over loose pants gathered at the ankle. Because Mrs. Bloomer wrote about this sensible garment, it became associated with her name, not that of its designer, Elizabeth Smith Miller. The press had great fun ridiculing bloomers and Mrs. Bloomer, and the style was a flop. But it paved the way for sensible gym clothes, swimsuits, and bicycle culottes that allowed women to move.

GIBSON GIRLS AND ARROW SHIRT MEN

Between 1870 and 1930, the number of female stenographers and typists increased from 5 to almost 92 percent of office staff. When women went to work, they wore a version of the Gibson Girl look—practical, comfortable, femininely slim skirts, white blouses, and tailored jackets. The beautiful Gibson Girl, with her hair piled high in an artful imitation of carelessness, was the creation of *Life* magazine artist Charles Dana Gibson, who captured the new spirit, spunk, humor, wistfulness, and grace of "the American Girl to all the world."

Her male equivalent was the Arrow Shirt Man, painted by German-born artist and illustrator J. C. Leyendecker. The Man was actually many men, all handsome and impeccably dressed. Leyendecker's models included future stars John Barrymore and Frederic March, and the artist's lifelong companion, Charles Beach. The Arrow Shirt Man, featured in illustrated ads from the end of World War I to 1930, was *the* fashion icon for men and a dreamboat to women, who sent him more fan mail than Rudolf Valentino.

THE SHOCKING MISS HEPBURN

When women took over male factory jobs during World War I, many wore pants and overalls. After the war, French designers kept the trousers trend alive, but a few Hollywood actresses, led by the eccentric, patrician Katharine Hepburn, transformed the public's disapproval to acceptance.

With her boyish figure and athletic grace, Hepburn looked fabulous in trousers, which she began wearing in college at Bryn Mawr, but her Hollywood studio bosses weren't charmed. Once, when she wore blue jeans to work, the men in charge had the jeans taken from her dressing room while she was on the set. Unruffled by the obvious ploy to get her into a skirt, Hepburn returned to the set in her underwear. Her trousers were quickly returned.

OUR NATIVE TONGUE

Jazz Age Slang: It's the Berries

Every generation creates slang, and most of it passes out of use with the next generation. But 1920s American slang remains surprisingly fresh. How many other generations have come up with so many ways to say "good things" and "good times," including the bee's knees, the cat's meow (or) pajamas, the berries, hotsy-totsy, keen, copacetic, and whoopee? More Jazz Age talk:

big cheese	a boss or VIP
breezer	a convertible car
Daddy	a rich boyfriend of any age
Dapper	a flapper's father
dead soldier	empty beer bottle
fire extinguisher	a chaperone
flat tire	bad date
gams	women's legs
handcuff	engagement ring
heebie-jeebies	the creeps
jake	okay, just fine
middle aisle	as a verb, to marry
ritzy	high class, elegant
sinker	doughnut
spifficated	intoxicated
Says you!	no way, unbelievable

LITTLE SHIRLEY'S CURLS AND CRINOLINES

As the Depression entered its worst days, Americans fell hard for a 6-year-old with sparkling eyes, bouncy blond curls, and dimples to die for. Shirley Temple, already a child star, became Hollywood's superstar with the release of *Bright Eyes* in 1934. In the process,

Cause of Death: Shaving Brush

A sad footnote in personal grooming history: In October 1921, Michael Francis Farley, a saloon keeper and former U.S. congressman, was killed by his shaving brush. A pathologist at New York's Bellevue Hospital recognized Farley's symptoms and administered anthrax serum, but it was too late. Farley died six hours after he arrived at the emergency room. His death was one of almost three dozen anthrax cases reported in the city over the previous year and a half.

The culprit? Contaminated horsehair bristles imported from Russia and Asia. Although New York City health officials had alerted the public to use only brushes made from badger hair or marked "sterilized," Farley apparently didn't get the message. The virulent anthrax strain he contracted was too far advanced for the serum, developed in the early 1900s, to be effective.

she saved 20th Century Fox from bankruptcy and inspired a fashion trend. Mamas coaxed their daughters' hair into tight ringlets (exactly 52 curls, as dictated by Shirley's mother) and dressed them in short, ruffled dresses and poufy petticoats—the look created by costumer Louis Royer. The trend waned, like Shirley's film career, with World War II, but endures on the stages of little girl beauty pageants.

FAKE STOCKINGS WITH SEAMS

At the 1939 New York World's Fair, Dupont introduced nylon stockings—sheer, strong, gossamer leggings that didn't sag and bunch up, cost less than silk, and made a gal's gams look great. Women went nuts for nylons but didn't have long to enjoy them. After the attack on Pearl Harbor, nylon production was diverted to parachutes, tents, and other military uses, and the importation of silk was ended. Unwilling to go back to baggy woven stockings, desperate but ingenious women colored their bare legs with tanning lotions and drew on fake seams with eyebrow pencil to duplicate the sexy nylon look.

MR. STRAUSS'S PANTS BECOME THE RAGE

The passage of denim jeans from the durable work clothing created by Morris Levi Strauss in the 1870s to today's ubiquitous garment of choice is usually associated with 1960s youth culture. But the blue jeans fashion actually started with teenagers in the 1940s and '50s. New jeans then were as stiff as a washboard. To get the starch out and shrink the jeans, kids would wear them while sitting in a tub of hot water, then batter the jeans against hard, dirty ground for an aged look. The popularity of jeans was hastened in the 1960s by the stonewashing process and by blending the denim with more pliable synthetic fabrics.

It was Jacob Davis, a tailor working in Reno, Nevada, who had the idea to add rivets to workpants to strengthen them. He joined with Levi Strauss to patent the design in 1873 and supervised the manufacture of the tough-as-nails jeans until his death in 1908.

PERMING AT HOME

The technique of curling human hair, patented by German inventor Karl Nessler in 1909, was a ray of sunshine for women with unfashionably straight hair, but required a visit to the beauty salon for a time-consuming and stinky process. The introduction of the home permanent, successfully exploited by the Toni Company founded by Yale graduate and former football tackle Richard Nelson Wishbone Harris in 1944, gave women an option that worked most of the time. (Wishbone was Harris's real name, as he constantly had to explain.)

Toni's famous advertising campaign featured attractive twin sisters with identical hairdos and asked the question, "Which twin has the Toni?" American women loved the look and the price; a Toni kit, complete with curlers, cost $2 at a time when salon perms ranged from $15 to $50.

SICKNESS AND DEATH

BATTLING ILLNESS AND INJURY HAS BEEN A CONSTANT
THEME IN OUR HISTORY, AND OUR FUNERAL CUSTOMS HAVE
CHANGED OVER TIME.

THE DREADED AGUE AND FLUX

The colonists didn't have proper medical terminology for many of the
illnesses that plagued them. The *ague* or *marsh fever* usually meant
malaria but could have been any number of insect-borne diseases,
including yellow fever (also known as *the black vomit*). Other major
illnesses were dysentery (*flux* or *bloody flux*), typhoid (*nervous fever*),
typhus (*jail fever*), hookworm, beri-beri, tuberculosis (*consumption*),
and smallpox. Persistent ulcerous sores and tumors were generally
classed as cancers. Tetanus could lead to gangrene (*mortification*) or
septicemia (*blood poisoning*). Heart disease was virtually unknown.

THE WAR ON SMALLPOX

Europeans inadvertently brought smallpox to the New World, where,
in the words of Massachusetts Governor Thomas Hutchinson, the
contagious disease "made terrible havock" among American Indians.
It wasn't much kinder to the colonists until Boston's Cotton Mather
read about inoculation in a British medical journal. Convinced
it would work against the pox, preacher Mather and Dr. Zabdiel
Boylston faced angry resistance from the medical community, local
authorities, and frightened citizens.

In spite of the fire bombing of Mather's house, the two men tested the procedure during a 1721 smallpox outbreak. They also kept clinical records and demonstrated statistically that inoculation dramatically reduced the death rate. Boylston and Mather's experiment is now regarded as a milestone in public health.

BLAME IT ON MODESTY

Nineteenth-century physicians, exclusively male, were prevented by Victorian standards of decency from examining women's naked bodies. As doctors wrested obstetrics away from traditional midwives, the code of modesty (a male doctor, sometimes wielding unsterile forceps, fumbled blindly beneath a tangle of sheets and his laboring patient's skirts) contributed to increasingly high rates of infant and maternal mortality. Recognizing the link between modesty and the rise in deaths and injuries in childbirth, some prominent physicians endorsed the training of female doctors to attend women and children, leading to the first American medical schools for women.

Patently Quack Medicines

There's no better example of the power of deceptive advertising than patent medicine, the worthless and sometimes harmful tonics, pills, and devices bought by Americans in the 19th and 20th centuries. Few patent medicines were actually patented, so the first fraud was in the name.

Without labeling requirements, gullible consumers didn't realize their "medicine" was no more than flavored ethyl alcohol, often spiked with cocaine, opium, or morphine. Marketers were free to make wild claims—"Greatest Remedy in the World!" (Lydia E. Pinkham's Vegetable Compound), "the draught that bids Consumption fly" (Dr. Swayme's Wild Cherry Tonic), and "Dropsy Cured! No Yankee Humbug!" (Broom's Anti-Hydropic Tincture).

THE HAZARDS OF WORK

Industrialization created new categories of illness caused by environmental contamination in factories, mines, and other work sites and gave rise to a new discipline, occupational medicine, with Dr. Alice Hamilton (1869–1970) of Indiana at its forefront. While teaching at Northwestern University in Chicago, she lived in Jane Addams's Hull House and saw firsthand the job-related health problems of poor workers. This experience turned her focus to industrial illnesses and toxicology. Her research into the effects of lead, arsenics, mercury, and other workplace toxins was groundbreaking.

In 1919, she was invited to become the Harvard Medical School's first female professor, but the headline for a New York newspaper's report—"A Woman on Harvard Faculty: The Last Citadel Has Fallen"—was premature. Before she could accept the offer, Dr. Hamilton had to agree not to enter the Faculty Club, ask for football tickets, or walk in the all-male commencement procession.

THE COSTLY EPIZOOTIC OF 1872

Late in September 1872, horses around Toronto, Canada, started falling ill. By mid-October the illness had reached New England and the upper Midwest. When this fast-moving epizootic—an epidemic in animals—played out in early spring, equine influenza had affected upwards of 99 percent of all horses in the country and crippled the economy. Farmers couldn't transport harvests. Trains didn't run because coal deliveries were halted. Ships couldn't load or unload cargo. Ambulance and tram service ceased; food markets were bare. During a devastating Boston fire, fire station horses were too weak to pull heavy water pumpers. Financial losses were huge, but the worst animal epidemic in U.S. history also brought expanded veterinary education and research, linking animals to the general public health and welfare.

MARCHING AGAINST POLIO

In a nationwide outbreak in 1916, polio took more than 7,000 lives, and the virulent, contagious, crippling disease continued to be the scourge of the century, disproportionately afflicting infants and children. In 1938, the March of Dimes was initiated by the newly established National Foundation for Infantile Paralysis to raise money, a dime at a time if necessary, to find a cure. Tens of thousands of mothers across the nation went door-to-door, soliciting pennies, nickels, and dimes that partly funded the breakthrough research of both Jonas Salk and Albert Sabin.

President Franklin Roosevelt, a polio victim, was a fervent supporter of the March of Dimes, and after his death in 1945, he was honored by having his image imprinted on newly minted dime coins.

MEDICINE ON THE BATTLEFIELD

The great irony of war is that amid so much death, life can be improved. This is especially true in emergency medicine, when urgent need tends to speed research and training in new treatments and delivery techniques that ultimately benefit civilians.

Civil War. The use of amputation led to improvements in anesthesia and cleanliness and to a better understanding of shock caused by blood loss. The syringe was invented. The first organized system of emergency treatment, including the introduction of four-wheeled ambulances, was developed by Dr. Jonathan Letterman.

Spanish-American War. For every death in battle, 14 American soldiers died of tropical diseases. Confirming a Cuban doctor's theory, Major Walter Reed launched a successful campaign to eradicate fever-bearing mosquitoes.

World War I. New methods were developed to treat tetanus, plastic surgery for facial and jaw wounds improved, and "triage" was integrated into emergency care.

World War II. Military doctors employed blood plasma to prevent shock, initiated large-scale use of penicillin and sulfa drugs, and developed drugs for malaria and pesticides to combat typhus.

Korean War. M.A.S.H. units (Mobile Army Surgical Hospitals) were deployed in battle zones, the first dialysis machine was used for shock-related kidney failure and hemorrhagic fever, and treatment of frostbite improved.

Vietnam War. Use of medical helicopters and Combat Support Hospitals saved many, but the military was slow to admit the effects of battlefield toxins such as Agent Orange. Psychological damage, earlier called shell shock and combat fatigue, was finally diagnosed as PTSD (post-traumatic stress disorder).

BURIED ALIVE

The Victorians' morbid fear of being buried alive was not entirely irrational at a time when coma states could easily be mistaken for death. It supposedly happened to Robert E. Lee's mother, who fortunately woke from a deep coma before her coffin was closed. Rumors abounded of people rescued at the last minute when they banged on the walls of their closed caskets. Edgar Allan Poe's terrifying 1844 short story "The Premature Burial" added to the general panic.

A "safety coffin" with an aboveground bell that could be rung by a chord inside the casket if a person awoke under ground was the logical choice for terrified Victorians who could afford it. A similar contraption allowed an entrapped person to hoist a flag. An early selling point for embalming and open-casket viewing was that this last look assured the living that the deceased was truly dead.

The Embalming Surgeon

At the start of the Civil War, President Lincoln became concerned with the problem of returning dead soldiers to their families for burial. As luck would have it, Dr. Thomas Holmes, a Columbia University–trained physician now known as "The Father of Modern Embalming," was in Washington and volunteered to embalm the body of the first Union casualty. Holmes, who developed his techniques from earlier work by European scientists, became the Union Army's first embalming surgeon, moving from battlefield to battlefield and by his count embalming more than 4,000 military dead.

Americans were slow to accept embalming after the war, mainly because of religious concerns about keeping bodies intact for burial, but morticians persisted. By the beginning of the 20th century, embalming was common practice, and old-time undertakers had evolved into funeral directors.

GOING OUT GREEN

In a return to early colonial custom, Americans in the 1990s began staging low-cost "green funerals," generally defined as burial without embalming, in a coffin of untreated wood, cardboard, or other biodegradable material. The ideal green cemetery—the nation's first opened in South Carolina in 1993—is maintained without pesticides and chemical fertilizers. Graves are often unmarked, locatable by GPS technology, or designated with a small stone.

Americans bury more than 100,000 tons of steel and a million tons of reinforced concrete in traditional cemeteries every year, so green funerals conserve natural resources. The green option also gives people more freedom of choice—a sentiment the colonists would appreciate.

Virginia Reels to Video Games

Our
Entertainments
and Pastimes

In some ways our forebears entertained themselves much as
we do today, and the way we gathered together, sang, danced,
and played sports naturally evolved over time. Pastimes
changed with new interests, attitudes, and technologies,
and the very idea of leisure time was redefined as radio and
television made their way into our homes.

ALL TOGETHER NOW

IN OUR EARLIEST DAYS, TAVERNS WERE THE PRIMARY GATHERING
PLACES FOR MEN, BUT MALES AND FEMALES ALIKE TOOK PART IN
"FROLICS," COMMUNAL HOUSE AND BARN RAISINGS, AND PICNICS.

ACTION CENTRAL

Colonial taverns usually served as inns, but drinking, eating, conversing, and game playing were the order of the day. Card players played whist (an early form of bridge) and other games, and usually placed bets under the radar. When singing broke out, the tunes of choice were the likes of "The Jolly Toper [heavy drinker]" and "Over the Hills and Far Away," both popular in the early 1700s. Yet the establishments were often the venue for much more: community meetings, circuit court sessions, business deals, and sundry other activities and events. (See also "Eat, Drink, and Plot a Revolution," page 32.)

Taverns had fare varying from cornmeal mush with molasses and johnnycakes in modest taverns to roast meats and fish in grander ones. As for clientele, the City Tavern in Philadelphia catered to the upper crust (including many of our Founding Fathers), while the New York tavern Dog's Head in the Porridge Pot was the rough-and-tumble province of longshoremen, sailors, and ladies of the night.

ORDINARY TIPPLING

The earliest word for a tavern was *ordinary,* an imported Briticism that would soon go by the board. Drinking in ordinaries wasn't entirely frowned upon even by the Puritans (who were quite fond of their nip o' grog), and only drunkenness was considered bad form.

In 1645 the General Court of Massachusetts decreed that excessive drinkers in taverns would be fined on a scale—"above the space of half an hour . . . 5s [shillings] for every such offence suffered" all the way up to "2s, 6d [sixpence] for sitting idle and continuing drinking above half an hour." Then there was the New England tithing-man, an elected city official whose job was to keep order at church services but who also went around poking his nose into the townspeople's business—including how much alcohol they consumed at the tavern.

"Cup o' Canary, Wench!"

Alongside the whiskey, beer, ale, and cider on a colonial tavern menu was a selection of drinks that might mystify the modern eye—yet the first six of the following potables can still be enjoyed today.

Alicante—red wine from the Alicante grape of Spain

Canary—sweet fortified wine later called Malmsey

Constantia—South African desert wine

Ebulum—Elderberry black ale

Kill-Devil—Jamaican rum

Malaga—Spanish dry sherry

Calibogus—spruce beer with rum

Fayal—wine from the Azores; a favorite of Thomas Jefferson

Flip—an eggnog-type drink seared with a hot poker

Metheglin—a type of mead (honey-based wine)

Switchel—ginger-water mixed with vinegar and molasses

OFF TO THE FROLIC

If there was any doubt that early America was an agricultural society, population distribution in the late 1600s and early 1700s tells the story: More than three-quarters of colonists lived on farms. Out of necessity, gatherings were often cooperative activities such as quilting frolics and house or barn raisings, usually followed by a period of socializing or entertainment. (*Frolic*, the early word for such a gathering, was supplanted in the mid-1700s by bee, long used to mean "a busy person.") At a typical frolic women young and old gathered to quilt, spin, or sew; their work and conversation (and no small measure of gossip) might end with a sing-along or the light supper they called "tea."

The husking frolic, an after-harvest ritual, was a perennial occasion from New England to the Louisiana Territory. In conservative areas, men, women, and children might sit in a circle to strip the husk from ear after ear of corn. In other places men turned husking into a heated contest, fueling their competitive spirit with swigs of whiskey or hard cider. As a rule, the frolic ended with a supper prepared by the women, followed by singing and dancing in the barn.

WORK, IMBIBE, WRESTLE

Husking frolics were a piece of cake compared to the communal work confined to men. House and barn raisings and the clearing of timber known as *log-rolling* (not to be confused with the river sport of lumberjacks) called for strong backs. At a raising it was common practice to set up only the timber-frames of the walls, and the placement of the ridgepole (the roof's highest horizontal timber) signaled that it was time to celebrate.

Wives and daughters prepared food, but the men usually were more interested in drinking and showing off their athletic prowess. The most daring climbed onto the ridgepole and performed death-defying stunts, while others paired off in a wrestling match. Wrestling was seen as a test of strength or a way to settle a score.

SONG AND DANCE

WE PUT OUR OWN STAMP ON MUSIC AND DANCE FROM THE
MOTHER COUNTRIES, AND IN DOING SO MADE A JOYFUL—
AND SOMETIMES MOURNFUL—NOISE.

THE SOUND OF MUSIC

The earliest American music came from the British Isles and the Continent, and slaves brought with them the sounds of Africa. Ballads, psalms (hymns), folk songs, and dance music were typically played on either violins (and rustic fiddles) or utes, and our music grew primarily from the Anglo and African music of the colonies.

The history of made-in-America genres is one of overlapping influences, subgenres, and popularization by recordings. Still, it's possible to put their origins in some semblance of chronological order, as below. Where are disco and punk, you ask? They're not from here: The former originated in France, the latter in Great Britain.

Negro spirituals—early 1800s
Minstrel music—early 1840s
Ragtime—1890s
Blues—early 1900s
Cajun music—early 1920s
Jazz—early 1920s
Country and western—mid-1920s
Swing, Big Band—mid-1920s
Gospel—late 1920s
Bluegrass—mid-1940s (first use of word)
Rhythm and blues—late 1940s

Rock and roll—1950s
Tejano— 1960s
Hip-hop—1980s

SHALL WE DANCE?

More colonists than not loved to dance. Depending on the venue—
a plantation house, a tavern, a slave camp—dance music was provided
by anything from a small orchestra to a single fiddle or fife.

In the 1770s, Virginia tutor Philip Fithian wrote of a ball given at
the plantation house known as Nomini Hall, noting the sequence of
the dances: ". . . first Minuets one Round; second Giggs [jigs]; third
Reels; and last of all Country-Dances." Among the dances of the day
were the Fop's Fancy (surely satirical) and the Sir Roger de Coverley,
the Scottish forerunner of the Virginia Reel.

Reels and quadrilles, the latter beginning with dancers standing
in a square rather than a circle, evolved into square dancing. The
Virginia Reel was also the lively ancestor of a slower-paced group
dance of the mid-20th-century: the stroll.

"BATTLE CRY OF FREEDOM": RUNAWAY HIT

One of the least-remembered American songwriters and music
publishers of the 19th century was also one of the most successful. Massachusetts-born George Frederick Root wrote close to 40
hits during the Civil War, often using the surname Wurzel (German
for "root"). His "Battle Cry of Freedom"—a hymn to Union troops
that more or less became the official campaign song for the Lincoln-
Johnson run in 1864—was so popular that his presses could barely
roll out enough sheet music to meet demand.

What's more, the Confederates fought back with their own version
of the song. The first two lines in the original Union version read,

The Union forever! Hurrah, boys, hurrah!
Down with the traitor, up with the star.

In the Rebel version, adapted by composer H. L. Schreiner and lyricist W. H. Barnes, the lines read,

Our Dixie forever! She's never at a loss;
Down with the eagle and up with the cross!

"TEN CENTS A DANCE"

In the Gold Rush days, dance halls in San Francisco charged men to dance with young women, and the custom soon spread to "taxi dancer" halls in Chicago, New Orleans, New York, and other large cities. A patron would buy a ticket for a dime, and the partner he selected danced with him for the length of a song. (As with taxis, customers were charged by time—hence the term *taxi dancer*.) At the end of the night, the dancer redeemed each of her tickets for a nickel; the other half went to the dance hall to pay overhead expenses. The tiring and often dispiriting life of the girls is echoed in the Rogers and Hart 1930 song "Ten Cents a Dance."

These establishments teetered on the edge of respectability even if they were well appointed and well run. Yet during taxi dancing's heyday in the Roaring Twenties, more than a few becoming young women jumped on the bandwagon, not least because they could earn much more than they could in a factory or shop.

ALL SHOOK UP

Rock and roll had a difficult birth in the 1950s, when juvenile delinquency and tension between the races were among the most worrisome concerns of the day. But despite the opposition of parents, religious groups, and social conservatives, the music that would come to be called rock and roll would not be kept at bay. Concerns of the day, and the establishment felt rhythm and blues was somehow inappropriate for white ears. In 1954 the blatantly suggestive hit "Work With Me, Annie," by Hank Ballard & the Midnighters, was rewritten as "Dance With Me Henry" and recorded by both Etta James and white singer Georgia Gibbs.

Teenagers refused to turn a deaf ear to what critics called the "jungle beat." And when Elvis Presley burst on the scene with his fusion of black, white, and country music, rock and roll exploded.

Amazingly, critics kept attacking rock and roll for decades, blaming it for everything from pregnancy to deafness. A Colorado preacher even claimed rock music was a communist plot—"an elaborate calculated scientific technique aimed at rendering a generation of American youth neurotic through nerve-jamming, mental deterioration, and retardation." Rock on?

My Band Name Is Weirder Than Your Band Name

By the mid-1990s, bands with names like Smashing Pumpkins, Counting Crows, and Hootie and the Blowfish had opened the door to increasingly creative nomenclature. Some of the groups in this list made a go of it, while others watched their drums fall silent after three or four gigs.

Afghanistan Banana Stand

Bertha's Mule

Buddy Whasisname and the Other Fellas

The Color Fred

The Disappointed Parents

Me First and the Gimmee Gimmees

The Naugahyde Chihuahuas

Question Mark and the Mysterians

She Stole My Beer

Stop Calling Me Frank

The Tortillas You Wanted

The Well I'm Sure I Left It There Yesterday Band

GAMES, GAMES, GAMES

MANY OF OUR GAMES AND SPORTS TESTIFY TO THE KNACK
OUR ANCESTORS HAD FOR TAKING THE TRADITIONS OF THE
OLD WORLD AND TURNING THEM INTO SOMETHING NEW.

PLAYING THE LOTTERY

Almost from the start the governments of all 13 colonies used lotteries to help finance public projects. A citizenry generally reluctant
to pay taxes welcomed the chance to win money, and in turn aided
the funding of schoolhouses, churches, bridges, jailhouses, and even
some institutions of higher learning built between 1636 and 1769:
Harvard, William and Mary, Yale, Princeton, King's College (later
Columbia), and Dartmouth.

GAMBLING IN THE COLONIES

Gambling—or gaming, as it was called—was always a part of American life, with men and women taking their chances on all sorts of
contests. Rich and poor alike placed bets, some astonishingly large.
Southerners in particular weren't afraid to "risk the farm": William
Byrd III, the son of a wealthy planter who was a member of the House
of Burgesses, was said to have sold 400 slaves to pay off the gambling
debts he incurred in 1765.

A wag of the time said that people in New Orleans would bet
on how long it took for bread dough to rise—an exaggeration, but
one with a grain of truth. Activities that invited betting throughout
the settled regions included backgammon, dice, foot races, fistfights,
boat races, and shuffleboard.

NELLIE BLY AND COMPANY

The most successful game of the late 1800s—Round the World with Nellie Bly—was based on a *New York World* journalist's 72-day steamship trip around the world. In an age when stunt journalism was common, 24-year-old Bly sought to beat the record of Phineas Fogg, the fictional hot-air-ballooning hero of Jules Verne's best-selling book *Around the World in Eighty Days* (1873). The public followed Bly's progress with bated breath, and soon the game replaying her journey was flying off store shelves.

A more enduring game arrived three decades later: Monopoly. The official line is that Charles Darrow, down and out in the Great Depression, invented the classic game bought by Parker Brothers. Truth be told, games based on real estate had been popular since the early 1900s, and one called The Landlord's Game predated Monopoly by 24 years. It featured 22 rental properties, 4 railroads, and a jail, exactly like the board game that became the biggest seller in the world.

BATTER UP!

Records of Americans playing "town ball" and "stick ball" in backyards and vacant lots date back to the late 18th century, but the first organized baseball game was played on the Boston Common in 1838. A game similar to British rounders was being played in the towns and cities of New York. How did these regional contests differ? Among other things, the so-called Massachusetts game fielded eight players on a rectangular field; the New York game fielded eleven players on a more diamond-shaped field.

Enter Alexander Cartwright. In 1845 this bookseller founded the New York Knickerbocker Base Ball Club, comprised of 28 gentlemen who met regularly to play the game. More important, Cartwright and three other members were the first to codify baseball rules. (Number

18: "No ace [run] or base can be made on a foul strike.") The single legacy from the Massachusetts game is the overhand, rather than underhand, pitch.

DIDN'T HAPPEN!
Abner Doubleday Invented Baseball

In 1905 Albert G. Spalding, the sporting goods manufacturer, attempted to prove that the game that had become America's national pastime had been invented on our soil. So he and his handpicked committee launched a search that brought in thousands of letters.

A letter from an elderly mining engineer from Colorado, Abner Graves, was much to the committee's liking. Graves wrote that in his youth he was friends with Abner Doubleday, who would go on to become a revered Civil War general. In 1839, Graves wrote, Doubleday coached a group of boys in a Cooperstown, New York, park in a new version of town ball with rules virtually identical to those of baseball at the turn of the 20th century.

Spalding's committee didn't bother to check the accuracy of the letter, and in 1907 proclaimed Doubleday as baseball's inventor. But research that began some 50 years later wholly discredited Mr. Graves's tall tale.

THE WACKY ST. LOUIS OLYMPICS

Had the 1904 Summer Olympics not coincided with the Louisiana Purchase Exposition in St. Louis, things might have gone better. As it was, the games vied for attention with exotic exhibits from around the world. So the man in charge, James Edward Sullivan of New York, attempted to hold at least one competition a day for the duration—and in those days, the Olympics lasted for almost four months.

The St. Louis Olympics mixed designated Olympic sports (including golf, tug-of-war, and roque, a U.S. version of croquet) with non-Olympic contests like cricket—all considered Olympic by Sullivan. No Olympic trials were held back then, and athletes could compete as individuals, not as part of a team.

The marathon told the story. Two Zulu tribesmen from the fair's Boer War exhibit decided to run, and Len Taunyane came in ninth, despite having been chased a mile off course by a pack of wild dogs. Cuban postman Felix Carbajal used scissors to turn his trousers into shorts and stopped along the way to eat some apples that proved rotten—although ill, he finished fourth. The gold medal for gall went to American runner Fred Lorz, who dropped out of the race at 9 miles, rode the next 11 in his manager's car, and got out in time to be the first runner to break the tape at the stadium. The American Athletic Union barred Lorz from competing for a year, after which he proved his mettle by winning the 1905 Boston Marathon.

FOOTBALL'S FEROCIOUS START

"It seems almost too good to believe that a president of one leading institution has common sense enough to do something to help rid college life of heathen cruelty and terror." So read the rather overheated letter of an alumnus of Columbia University when his alma mater temporarily abolished football in 1905. Columbia was only one of the schools to ban a game so brutish it had led to serious injury and even death. Players on the receiving end of tight "mass momentum" offenses could end up with broken bones or worse, and uniforms offered little or no protection (the leather headwear of the time was so soft it could be folded and stuffed into a back pocket).

As the public outcry grew louder, President Theodore Roosevelt called a conference of sport leaders in October 1905—among them Walter Camp, the former Yale captain who devoted himself to reshaping the game and came to be considered the father of American football. Over the next few years, intercollegiate rules committees met in various states, making changes that opened up the game with the forward pass and other innovations. Out of these committees came the National Collegiate Athletic Association (NCAA), founded in 1910.

The more safety-conscious rules were also applied to professional football, which had gotten off the ground around the turn of the century.

Premier Professionals

Some of the teams and athletes who took the first professional championships in American sports have gone to the great beyond, but they all had their shining day in the sun. The following is a chronological list.

U.S. Open (tennis), men's—Richard D. Sears (1881)

U.S. Open (tennis), women's—Ellen Hansel (1887)

U.S. Open (golf), men's—Horace Rawlins (1895)

World Series—Boston Americans (1903)

Indianapolis 500 speed race—Ray Harroun (1911)

Professional Golf Association (PGA)—Jim Barnes (1916)

National Hockey League (NHL) Stanley Cup, Canadian team— Toronto Arenas (1918)

NHL Stanley Cup, American team—New York Rangers (1928)

PGA Masters Tournament—Horton Smith (1934)

National Basketball Association—Philadelphia Warriors (1947)

U.S. Open (golf), women's—Babe Didrickson Zaharias (1948)

NASCAR Nationwide Series—Ray Klapak (1949)

Ladies Professional Golf Association—Beverley Hanson (1955)

National Football League Superbowl—Green Bay Packers (1967)

North American Soccer League—Atlanta Chiefs (1968)

Major Soccer League—D.C. United (1996)

NINTENDO'S LOOK BACK

After *Pong* launched electronic gaming in 1972 and *Pac-Man* won over millions of fans in 1980, Nintendo of America introduced the arcade game *Donkey Kong* in 1981. Making a bow in the breakthrough game was a character who would become king of the hill—Mario, an Italian plumber who lived in the Mushroom Kingdom. With sales of over 200 million, the Mario and Super Mario series rank among the best selling games of all time.

Nintendo was founded in Kyoto, Japan, in 1889 to make a traditional Japanese card game by hand—Hanafuda, which is played with 48 small, numberless cards divided into 12 suits representing the months of the year (the suits are distinguished by colorful plants and flowers rather than symbols). In 2007 Nintendo brought out a Mario version of the cards, with the feisty plumber peeking out from behind a pine tree or frolicking in red clover. Whether such a game can catch the attention of die-hard video buffs is uncertain—but could Nintendo's loving nod to its past start a trend?

Brawn, Brains

Four universities lucky enough to have produced Superbowl-winning quarterbacks have an even bigger feather in their collective cap: a graduate who went on to become president of the United States. Fans can decide whether the geographic distribution of the schools means anything: one in the East, one in the West, and two in the Midwest.

And the winners are:

University of Michigan. Tom Brady; Gerald Ford

Stanford University. John Elway and Jim Plunkett; Herbert Hoover

United States Naval Academy. Roger Staubach; Jimmy Carter

Miami University of Ohio. Ben Rothlisberger; Benjamin Harrison

READING MATTER

BY THE LATE 1700S, MOST AMERICANS WERE LITERATE,
AND THERE WAS NO SHORTAGE OF BOOKS AND PUBLICATIONS
TO KEEP THEM OCCUPIED.

THE RISE OF LITERACY

The growth of newspapers and magazines coincided with rising
literacy rates. Between 1725 and 1800 the number of newspapers
published in the colonies grew from 4 to 197. Between 1755 and 1800
the number of magazines went from 2 to 14.

Historians estimate that by 1800 virtually 100 percent of adult
males and at least 90 percent of adult women in New England could
read and write—a higher literacy rate than in any other colonies or in
England. (The high rates are partly explained by the importance the
early Puritans placed on Bible reading.) In the South, around two-
thirds of adult males and one-third of adult females were literate.

THE ASTONISHING MRS. CHILD

What *didn't* Lydia Maria Child write? She founded *The Juvenile
Miscellany,* the nation's first periodical for children, in 1826. She
wrote two books devoted to domestic life: *The American Frugal
Housewife* (1829) and *The Mother's Book* (1831). And as a poet, Child
wrote *"Over the River and Through the Woods,"* later set to music and
as familiar to us today as it was in the 19th century.

The socially conscious woman born Lydia Francis in Medford,
Massachusetts, in 1802 also made her mark as editor of the weekly
National Anti-Slavery Standard and author of *That Class of Americans*

Called Africans (1833), a key work of the abolition movement. Her *History of the Condition of Women* (1835) foreshadowed the feminist movement and was praised by suffragist leader Elizabeth Cady Stanton as an invaluable resource in the fight for women's rights.

OUR NATIVE TONGUE

The Final Word on OK

Conventional wisdom once held that the word H. L. Mencken called "the most successful of all Americanisms"—*OK*, alternately spelled O.K. or okay—was drawn from the nickname of President Martin Van Buren: Old Kinderhook. But while Van Buren's campaign of 1840 popularized OK, the word had already found a place in the language.

Abbreviating words or spelling them facetiously became a major fad in the 1830s; *NG* stood for "no go," *SP* for "small potatoes." The term *all right* became "oll wright," or *OW,* while *all correct* became "oll korrect," or *OK.*

OK separated from the pack when Van Buren's supporters formed the O.K. (Old Kinderhook) Club during his failed second campaign. The publicity garnered by the club elevated the use of the word that would eventually spread to every corner of the globe.

TWO MADE-IN-AMERICA GENRES

Edgar Allan Poe deviated from his darkly Gothic, romantic tales and poems when he wrote "The Murders in the Rue Morgue," a short story published in *Graham's Magazine* in 1841. It was something completely different—a story about a rational private investigator, C. Auguste Dupin, who solves a complicated murder mystery. It was also the beginning of a new genre: detective fiction. Among the legions of European and American detectives who followed in Dupin's footsteps were Sherlock Holmes (created by Sir Arthur Conan Doyle), Hercule Poirot (Agatha Christie), Philip Marlowe (Raymond Chandler), and, more recently, Dr. Kay Scarpetta (Patricia Cornwell).

If Poe is a household name, the man who jump-started science fiction is known mainly to sci-fi buffs. When New Yorker Hugo

Gernsback, a science magazine publisher, devoted a 1923 issue to "scientifiction," he started the Americanization of a genre that had mainly been the province of the English (think H. G. Wells) and French (Jules Verne). The response to the issue was so overwhelming that Gernsback launched the science fiction magazine *Amazing Stories.* Gernsback is remembered as the father of science fiction and is the namesake of sci-fi's highest honor, the Hugo Award.

THE BOBBSEY TWINS AND FRIENDS

It's hard to believe anyone would look down on the endearing Nancy Drew, but the literary establishment of the early 20th century almost considered her a threat to society. Worse, her partners in crime were the Bobbsey Twins, the Hardy Boys, Tom Swift, and a plethora of lesser-known cohorts. Books of the time were expected to deliver some kind of morality lesson, but series books such as these were designed for pure entertainment—leading to, in the words of critics with upturned noses, "intellectual torpor."

Edward Stratemeyer didn't get the message. In 1905 he founded the Stratemeyer Syndicate, a packager of juvenile and adult series books. Six years before, he had launched the wildly successful Rover Boys series (1899–1926), which served as the model for the books the syndicate churned out for 77 years. That ghostwriters came and went and often shared the same pen names was a closely guarded secret.

The cat was let out of the bag in 1980, a half-century after Stratemeyer's death. When the publisher Grosset & Dunlap got wind that Stratemeyer's daughters were going to give cash cow Nancy Drew to publisher Simon & Schuster, they sued for breach of contract and copyright infringement. During the trial, Iowa-born journalist Mildred Wirt Benson came out of the closet as Nancy Drew author Carolyn Keene. Benson had penned 23 of the first 25 Nancy Drew books—an accomplishment that in 2001 earned her a special Edgar Award from the Mystery Writers of America.

STAGE AND SCREEN

IN THE 19TH CENTURY, WE FINALLY CREATED OUR OWN THEATRI-
CAL TRADITIONS. IN THE NEXT CENTURY WE INTRODUCED THE
WORLD TO AN ART FORM THE LIKES OF WHICH HAD NEVER BEEN
SEEN BEFORE: THE HOLLYWOOD MOVIE.

THEATER'S UPS AND DOWNS AND UPS

Professional theater in the colonies began with the arrival of the
Englishman Lewis Hallam and his itinerant troupe of actors in 1752.
In the mid-1800s another European import gained a following—bur-
lesque, which began with females in male roles parodying politics
and culture (*il Travatore* became *Kill Travatore*) but degenerated into
a tawdry bump-and-grind spectacle. Then came an all-American,
family-friendly form of theater with universal appeal: vaudeville.

Impresarios searching out the middle ground between high and
low entertainment were behind this cleaner variety show format. The
two most influential were Benjamin F. Keith and Edward F. Albee II
(grandfather of award-winning playwright Edward Albee). The lavish
Bijou Theater that Keith built in Boston in 1884—with its "fixed
policy of cleanliness and order"—was the first of many vaudeville
palaces that would be the jewels of a nationwide vaudeville circuit.

In quick succession the acts served up comedians, singers,
dancers, mind readers, escape artists (Houdini among them), con-
tortionists—you name it. Before it began to wane in the late 1920s,
vaudeville had primed performers such as Milton Berle, Jack Benny,
Judy Garland (of the Gumm Sisters), Groucho Marx, Mae West, and
Will Rogers for careers that would make them legends.

Rotten Tomatoes for the Cherry Sisters

The corn-fed Cherry Sisters of Iowa called their vaudeville act *Something Good, Something Sad.* Audiences and critics called it something atrocious. Addie, Effie, Lizzie, Jessie, and Ella were not only talentless but came off as a bunch of morally superior hall monitors. A strong religious and patriotic vein ran through the act's songs, skits, dances, and morality plays, and in one scene Jessie was suspended from a cross. Their performances were greeted with a hail of catcalls and rotten vegetables, and the reviews that followed leaned heavily on satire and sarcasm.

Still, the sisters were no shrinking violets. In 1898 the *Des Moines Leader* ran a review describing the sisters as "three creatures surpassing the witches in Macbeth in general hideousness . . . the mouths of their rancid features opened like caverns and [the singing] sounded like the wailings of damned souls . . ." True, the stocky sisters were anything but pretty, but this was a bit much. They sued the newspaper for "false and malicious" libel. Both the Polk County Court and the Iowa Supreme Court ruled in the newspaper's favor, and *Cherry v. Des Moines Leader* is viewed as a pivotal decision confirming the press's right to fair comment and critical analysis.

The sisters stopped performing in 1903 but could die knowing they played Broadway. In 1896, Oscar Hammerstein I put them on the stage in a "so bad it's good" gamble that paid off handsomely for both the sisters and the impresario.

THE ASTOR PLACE RIOT

A feud between a robust American superstar and an effete English actor ended in the Astor Place Opera House riot of May 10, 1849, described a century later by book reviewer H. I. Block as "an uprising of indignant American patriots against 'foreigners.'"

Philadelphia-born Edwin Forrest enthralled audiences with his muscular performances of Shakespeare. London-born William C. Macready toured the United States in 1843–1844 and later thanked his huge audiences by calling them "essentially ignorant or vulgar." The two men had a long-running feud, and when Macready sailed to New York to play *Macbeth* at Astor Place, the stage was set for battle.

On Macready's opening night of May 7, Forrest, who had pointedly played *Macbeth* in the weeks before Macready's arrival, held forth in *The Gladiator* (by American playwright Robert Montgomery Bird) at another theater.

The press had drummed up the rivalry, and young toughs from the Bowery meant to put Macready in his place. At his first performance the boys in the peanut gallery greeted him with hisses, boos, and missiles. Three days later, rowdiness in the theater led to the hecklers being kicked outside, where a crowd of over 10,000 people had gathered. Louts began to throw stones through the theater windows, and as the police arrived, the crowd turned their volleys on the law. The police opened fire, killing not only perpetrators but also innocent bystanders. Accounts number the dead at up to 30 and well over a hundred injured, making the Astor Place Riot one of the worst tragedies in the history of American theater.

THE BROADWAY MUSICAL TAKES OFF

By the mid-1800s American theater boasted plenty of musical entertainments, but none like the extravaganza that debuted in New York on September 12, 1866: *The Black Crook,* in which the title character, Herzog, a bad apple who practices black magic, kidnaps Rodolphe, the boyfriend of the pretty Amina, at the behest of the lustful and manipulative Count Wolfenstein. The convoluted melodrama lasted for five and a half hours, but its out-of-this-world features—mechanical scenery, winsome soloists, live animals, and a moonlit grotto where ballerinas in flesh-colored tights jumped and twirled—made it the most profitable musical of its time.

The next major milestone came in 1927 with the arrival of Jerome Kern and Oscar Hammerstein II's *Show Boat,* the first musical to tell a solid story through words and music—this one set in the ripe-for-drama Mississippi riverboat culture. The Broadway musical reached its zenith with *Oklahoma!,* the Rogers and Hammerstein smash that opened in March 1943 and ran for 2,212 performances, connecting music, dance, and story in a fresh and compelling way. And if the song *Oklahoma!* hadn't been added during out-of-town tryouts and wowed the crowds, the show would have retained its original name: *Away We Go!*

AN INVASION OF TALENT

Many of Hollywood's earliest VIPs were immigrants. Producer Louis B. Meyer, who invented the studio system, was born in Belarus. Director Frank Capra, who won three Oscars in five years, beginning with *It Happened One Night* (1934), was Sicilian. From Vienna came Billy Wilder, the director, screenwriter, and producer who gave us such classics as *Sunset Boulevard* (1950), *Some Like It Hot* (1959), and *The Apartment* (1960).

Foreign actors lent a certain allure to films that made them all the more escapist. Hedy Lamarr moved from Austria to Hollywood in 1938. Billed as the world's most beautiful woman, she was best known for her 10-minute nude scene in the Czech film *Ecstasy* (1933). Berlin-born Marlene Dietrich set the screen ablaze with her sensuality, while Ingrid Bergman of Sweden radiated strength. Romanian immigrant Edward G. Robinson brought gruffness to a new level, and Hungarian Peter Lorre was a master of the sinister. Suave Charles Boyer helped cement the reputation of the French lover (though his famous line to Hedy Lamarr in the 1938 film *Algiers*—"Come with me to the casbah"—never made it from trailer to final cut), and Omar Sharif, an Egyptian of Lebanese descent, set female hearts aflutter with his Oscar-nominated performance in *Lawrence of Arabia* (1962).

GIMMICK-O-RAMA

With television cutting into movie attendance in the 1950s, film studios tried almost anything to lure viewers away from the small screen. Gimmicks moved beyond expensive new projection techniques like Cinerama and Panavision to the physical. Moviegoers greeted Smell-o-Vision with so big a yawn that it lasted for exactly one film: *Scent of Mystery* (1950). The goal of the horror flick *The Tingler* (1959) was to shock—literally. Columbia Pictures supplied movie houses with wired contraptions that would make some movie seats deliver mild electric shocks. (Among the tag lines were "Amazing NEW TERROR

DIDN'T HAPPEN!
Oscars to Ian Hunter and Robert Rich

In 1954 the Academy Award for best screenplay went to Ian McLellan Hunter for *Roman Holiday*. In 1957 the best screenplay Oscar went to Robert Rich for *The Brave One*. Thing is, Hunter didn't write that screenplay, and Rich didn't even exist. Both names were pseudonyms used by world-renowned Dalton Trumbo—the first borrowed from a screenwriter friend in England, the second made up.

This strange state of affairs began in 1947, when the House on Un-American Activities Committee (HUAC, whose job was to root out and expose Communists) went after film industry workers who were suspected of planting pro-Communist or anti-American messages in motion pictures. Many who refused to testify or name names not only landed in jail but were also blacklisted by the studios.

One of the most defiant was Trumbo. Beginning in 1950 he served 11 months in jail for contempt of Congress. After his release he moved to Mexico, then back to California to write anonymously. Not until 1960 was he once again credited for his screenplays: *Spartacus and Exodus*, released 10 weeks apart in the first year of the new decade.

And the orphan Oscar statuettes? The first was given to Trumbo in 1975. The second was presented posthumously to Trumbo's wife, Cleo, in 1993 (Trumbo died in 1976).

Highest Grossing Films

When a movie studio proclaims that the latest blockbuster is one of the highest-grossing films of all time, take it with a grain of salt. Such rankings are legitimate only when based on gross domestic receipts in inflation-adjusted dollars—like the top ten listed below. (Note: The grosses for numbers 1 and 10 were from multiple releases.)

1. *Gone With the Wind* (1939)

2. *Star Wars* (1977)

3. *The Sound of Music* (1965)

4. *E.T.: The Extra-Terrestrial* (1982)

5. *The Ten Commandments* (1956)

6. *Titanic* (1997)

7. *Jaws* (1975)

8. *Doctor Zhivago* (1965)

9. *The Exorcist* (1973)

10. *Snow White and the Seven Dwarfs* (1937)

Device [the long-forgotten "Percepto"] Makes You A Living Participant in the FLESH-CRAWLING ACTION!" and "BRING YOUR DATE AND WATCH HER TINGLE!")

What did succeed to an extent was 3-D, which made a new-and-improved comeback in the 1990s. In the '50s, viewers had to don cheap cardboard glasses, which worked well enough to make viewers duck from onscreen projectiles in films like *House of Wax* and *It Came From Outer Space* (both released in 1953), but not nearly well enough to change the face of moviemaking.

RADIO AND TV

RADIO WAS ONE OF THE MIRACLES OF THE JAZZ AGE—
BUT AS AL JOLSON WORDED IT, AMERICANS OF THE 1920S
"AIN'T SEEN NOTHIN' YET!"

AMERICANS TUNE IN

Commercial broadcasting began on November 2, 1920, when radio station KDKA of Pittsburgh transmitted news reports of Warren G. Harding's election as president. The station had the airwaves to itself for ten months before additional independent stations began popping up. At first most people listened on homemade crystal radios, but by the mid-1920s factory-made radios were flooding the market.

By the end of the decade, every third household in the United States owned a radio, and the first networks—National Broadcasting Company (NBC) and Columbia Broadcasting System (CBS) were leasing transcontinental telephone circuits to link affiliated stations. Almost overnight, it seemed, Americans could enjoy comedy and drama and news programs in their living rooms. Radio also introduced them to another 20th-century phenomenon—the commercial. Advertisers not only bought airtime but also created their own programs, including the *A & P Gypsies,* the *Bell Telephone Hour,* and even the *Fleischmann's Yeast Hour,* which turned crooner Rudy Vallee into one of the biggest stars of the era.

MOTHER OF ALL SOAPS

As radio cast about for ways to keep people listening, a new kind of program came along: daily, 15-minute serial dramas with recurring characters who experienced the joys and sorrows of real life. WGN Radio of Chicago hatched the idea and asked a young actress/writer named Irna Phillips to create a show. Phillips delivered *Painted Dreams,* a look into the lives of an Irish-American family and their widowed matriarch: Mother Moynihan, played by Phillips herself. The show debuted on October 20, 1930, and *voila!*—a new genre arrived. The shows would later be called "soap operas" because most were sponsored by Proctor & Gamble.

Phillips would also write the first soap for TV: *These Are My Children* (1949). But nothing outshone her show *The Guiding Light,* which premiered on the radio in 1937, moved to TV in 1952, and became the longest-running soap opera in history. Other shows Phillips created or co-created include *As the World Turns* (1956), *Another World* (1964), and *Days of Our Lives* (1965).

To call Phillips eccentric would be kind. She killed off the characters of actors she didn't like and once fired an actress because she couldn't stand the way the newcomer poured her coffee. But a difficult personality couldn't keep the Chicago-born creative dynamo from going down in history as the mother of the soap opera.

"LIVE FROM STUDIO ONE"

Television brought live plays into American living rooms in the late 1940s. The longest running of these so-called anthology dramas, *Studio One* (1948–1958), had a yearlong radio "try-out" before moving to CBS Television. What shows like *Studio One, Playhouse 90, Philco Television Playhouse* (called *Goodyear Television Playhouse* every other week, as it alternated sponsors), and *Kraft Television Theater* had in common was some of the best playwriting around. All of the teleplays lasted an hour, with the exception of those on *Playhouse 90* (1956–1961), named for its 90-minute format.

A number of plays written for television had continuing success down the line. Among these productions and playwrights were:

Marty. Paddy Chayefsky; *Philco Television Playhouse,* 1953. The film adaptation of the teleplay about a lonely man who finds love won the Oscar for best picture in 1955.

Twelve Angry Men. Reginald Rose; *Studio One,* 1954. This courtroom drama was adapted for film in 1957 and played to critical acclaim on Broadway in 2004.

Judgment at Nuremberg. Abby Mann; *Playhouse 90,* 1957. Mann, who based the drama on the post–World War II war crimes trial in Germany, adapted his teleplay for the big screen in 1961.

Days of Wine and Roses. J. P. Miller; *Playhouse 90,* 1958. The movie version of this harrowing drama of a married couple's descent into alcoholism was released in 1962.

VARIETY IS THE SPICE OF . . .

Television variety shows were the direct descendants of vaudeville, and in the 1950s they were performed live. Comedian Milton Berle took *Texaco Star Theater* from radio to TV as Uncle Miltie, who frequently donned crazy costumes as he presided over a parade of singers, dancers, and the cream-of-the-crop comics. The show was so popular that it caused sales of TV sets to soar. *Your Show of Shows,* with gags supplied by writers like Mel Brooks and Woody Allen, made Sid Caesar and his cohost Imogene Coca two of the most popular stars of TV's so-called Golden Age. Among their characters were Doris and Charlie Hickenlooper, but Caesar alone assumed the persona of Somerset Winterset, Giuseppe Marinara, and other oddballs.

A mixed bag followed, including the long-running *Carol Burnett Show* (1967–1978), the shorter-lived *Smothers Brothers Comedy Hour* (1967–1969), and *The Sonny and Cher Comedy Hour* (1971–1974). All the while, *The Ed Sullivan Show* had been a rock, keeping television audiences amused from 1948 to 1971 with every type of entertainment imaginable: comedians, opera stars, circus acts, and rock singers who would practically sell their mothers for a booking.

EARLY MORNING, LATE NIGHT

It couldn't have been the inconvenient time slots that made NBC's *Today* and *Tonight* two of the longest-running television shows in history (third and seventh, respectively). It was more likely the laid-back style of their hosts and a format that mixed talk, entertainment, and serendipity. *Today* hit the airwaves for the first time on January 14, 1952 with an unassuming, bespectacled host named Dave Garroway—one of a new breed with the relaxed air of the guy next door.

Steve Allen was the first host of the *Tonight* show—which has had only four hosts since, thanks to a 1962 to 1992 run by showbiz legend Johnny Carson. When *Tonight* premiered on September 24, 1954, Allen was already well known as a quick-witted raconteur who played the piano and composed songs at the drop of a hat (no doubt doing his vaudeville-performer parents proud). Some TV historians give Allen credit for inventing the talk show format.

Presenting J. Fred Muggs

NBC's *Today* was slow to get off the ground after its debut in January 1952. The performer who boosted the ratings a year later was a multitalented chimp named J. Fred Muggs. The 13-week-old primate started out wearing diapers on air and graduated to playsuits. As Dave Garroway's cohost, J. Fred somersaulted, roller-skated, played the piano, and finger-painted (one of his paintings graced the cover of *Mad* magazine in 1958).

The older J. Fred grew, the more ornery he became. He even bit a guest, the singer Martha Raye. But J. Fred's 1957 departure from *Today* wasn't the end of his career: A decade later he worked a 5-year gig at Busch Gardens in Tampa, Florida. The former TV star retired in Florida with species-correct girlfriend Phoebe B. Beebe, who had occasionally joined J. Fred on *Today.*

ASSORTED AMUSEMENTS

FUN PARKS AND SHOWMEN LIKE P. T. BARNUM DID MUCH TO
AMUSE US, AND A LATE-1800S FLOWERING OF MUSEUM GOING
THREW ENLIGHTENMENT INTO THE MIX.

A DAY AT THE TROLLEY PARK

The last decade of the 19th century saw the emergence of "trolley parks" on the outskirts of cities. Electric trolley lines made it possible to carry fun seekers to sites such as Ponce de Leon Park in Atlanta and Idora Park in Youngstown, Ohio. These and other parks offered everything from mechanized rides to eateries to animal exhibitions and sideshows.

The grandfather of the modern amusement park was Coney Island, located on a five-mile stretch of sand dunes off the southeast tip of Brooklyn. Starting in 1897, park goers from far and wide could get their thrills at Steeplechase Park's mechanical steeplechase ride (a simulated horse race) or walk over to Luna Park and brave a scary but exhilarating swoop down the Helter Skelter slide. Dreamland allowed a stroll through the streets of Cairo, a visit to an Eskimo village, a look at the fall of Pompeii, and even a plunge "20,000 leagues under the sea."

The new electric lighting turned Coney Island into a nighttime fantasyland. "Tall towers . . . suddenly broke forth in electric outlines and gay rosettes of color," observed author and Mark Twain pal Albert Bigelow Paine, "as the living spark of light traveled hither and thither, until the place was transformed into an electric garden, of such a sort as Aladdin had never seen."

A DAY AT THE MUSEUM

In 1773, the Charlestown Library Society in South Carolina opened a museum whose purpose was to enlighten the public in the basics of agriculture and herbal medicines. (Today, as the Charleston Museum, it preserves the cultural and natural history of the city and region.) The painter Charles Willson Peale followed in 1786 with the Peale Museum, making natural history and technological objects accessible to the public. In 1869, New York's American Museum of Natural History brought natural history to life with dioramas, three-dimensional re-creations of the natural habitats of birds and animals and the village life of ancient peoples. But it was British mineralogist and chemist James Smithson who founded what would become the largest museum complex in America: the Smithsonian Institution, the first museum of which was the U.S. National Museum in 1846.

Museums began to bring fine art to the public with the opening of the Pennsylvania Academy of Fine Arts in 1805, also founded by Peale. New York artists and intellectuals teamed with businessmen and financiers to found the Metropolitan Museum of Art in 1872. A century later, art museums countrywide were displaying works not only of the European grand masters but also of artists who forged America's two great art movements: the Ash Can school of the early 20th century, whose painters pulled no punches when portraying real life; and mid-century Abstract Expressionism, the first American movement to exert influence worldwide.

THE WORLD OF P. T. BARNUM

P. T. Barnum was the greatest showman America ever produced. Over the course of a career that lasted from 1835 until his death in 1891, he toured the country exhibiting the 11½-foot-tall Jumbo the elephant and 33-inch-tall General Tom Thumb. He brought over Jenny Lind, "the Swedish Nightingale," to perform and win hearts at concerts across the nation. And his museums in Philadelphia and New York lured millions. But in a few cases, Barnum owed your great-great-great-grandparents an apology. His most blatant hoaxes centered on:

Joice Heth. In 1835 Barnum bought the rights to exhibit this elderly black woman and billed her as the 161-year-old former nurse of George Washington. When interest waned, he started a rumor that Heth was an automaton, and people flocked to his museum to figure out whether Heth (actually 80) was human or mechanical.

The Feejee Mermaid. The mummy of a mermaid from the South Pacific caused a stir from the moment it arrived in New York with Dr. J. Griffin of the British Lyceum of Natural History. Barnum urged Griffin to allow him to exhibit the mermaid at his American Museum, and the crowds followed. In truth, Griffin was Barnum's friend Levi Lyman, and the mermaid was the upper body of a monkey grafted onto the body of a fish.

The Cardiff Giant. A 10-foot-tall petrified man unearthed at a farm outside Cardiff, New York, was said to be one of the giants mentioned in Genesis 6:4: "There were giants in the earth in those days." He was really the creation of hoaxer George Hull, who made a quick buck when a group of businessmen bought the so-called Cardiff Giant to exhibit it. Barnum offered them a handsome fee for the giant, and when they refused, he had a plaster replica made and exhibited it as the original.

As co-owner of the Barnum & Bailey Circus, the showman was strictly legit. He was the first to move a circus by train, and when Barnum & Bailey merged with Ringling Brothers, the result was the "Greatest Show on Earth."

Up in the Air: Funambulists

Tightrope walkers of the 19th century, some of whom went from town to town, were called funambulists, from the Latin *funis* (rope) and *ambulare* (to walk). The most famous was the Frenchman Charles Blondin, who on June 30, 1859, walked a rope strung across the gorge below Niagara Falls time after time. With each pass, as Blondin donned a blindfold, pushed a wheelbarrow, or carried a man on his back, the hearts of onlookers beat faster.

Another funambulist was all but forgotten except in Corsicana, Texas, the small town where he appeared one day in 1884. How the stranger managed to string a rope between two buildings on the main street is lost to history, but other details have survived in an early account:

"The unusual part [was that] this man had a Peg Wood leg. He attempted to cross this wire on one leg and a wood peg with a cook stove tied on his back." Carrying a long bar for balance, the man stepped out on the rope above the crowd that had gathered and made it to the halfway point before he lost his balance and fell.

As he lay in the street, his chest crushed by the stove, a group of onlookers picked him up and carried him to a nearby hotel. There a doctor and an evangelist preacher attended the man, who refused to give his name. But as he neared death, the man said to the doctor, "I wish to talk to a Jew." A Jewish merchant was called (the town had no rabbi at the time), who asked the stranger to "repeat a Certain prayer," which "he did in excellent Hebrew."

No one ever learned the man's name, but a small tombstone engraved with the words "Rope Walker" stands in Corsicana's Hebrew Cemetery to this day.

THE OTHER WILD BILL

As Wild Bill Cody (also known as Buffalo Bill for his prowess as a buffalo hunter), William Frederick Cody shaped the world's perception of the Old West. His traveling Wild West show (1883–1913) idealized historic events, gunslinging, and the lives of cowboys and American Indians. Cody also roped the marshal and dime-novel hero Wild Bill Hickok into the act.

A third Bill with a Wild West show dubbed himself Pawnee Bill—and with good reason. Gordon William Lillie of Kansas became friendly with the Pawnee who had camped near his town and ended up following them to Pawnee, Oklahoma, where he taught school on the reservation and acted as an interpreter. When Lillie married in 1886, his friend Blue Hawk sold land outside Pawnee to the couple.

In 1889 Gordon and his wife, Mary, formed Pawnee Bill's Historical Wild West Indian Museum and Encampment Show, which was good enough to tour Europe. Back in the States, Gordon tried to increase the show's earnings by adding Arab jugglers, Chinese and Japanese acts, and a well-known performer called Mexican Joe. In 1908 the show merged with Cody's to become Buffalo Bill's Wild West and Pawnee Bill's Far East Show, and Gordon finally found success. In 1913 Pawnee Bill retired to his ranch and invested in banking, real estate, and oil—not bad for the "other Bill" in the picture.

Index

A

Abolition, 44, 52, 56
Adams, John, 33, 44, 48–49
African Americans, 35, 43–44, 57, 73, 74, 77
Allen, Steve, 164
America First Committee, 67–70
American Indians, 19–20, 51, 59, 132
Amusement parks, 165
Anthrax, 130
Antietam, Battle of, 55
Appomattox Court House, 56
Armed forces. See specific wars or operations
Arrow Shirt Men, 128
Art, colonial, 24
Articles of Confederation, 40
Astor, John Jacob, 80, 105
Astor Place riot, 156–57

B

Baby Boom, 119
Bacon's Rebellion, 23
"Barbara Frietchie" (Whittier), 57
Barbed wire, 89
Barnum, P. T., 166–67
Baseball, 147–48
Bell, Alexander Graham, 100
Berlin Blockade, 71
Billings, Cornelius Kingsley Garrison, 122–23
Biofuels, 90
Bird, Mark, 79

Blondin, Charles, 168
Bloomers, 127
Blue jeans, 131
"Blue laws," 20–21
Bly, Nellie, 147
Board games, 147
Boarding houses, 109
Bonaparte, Jerome, 114–15
Bonsack, James, 97
Borlaug, Norman, 90
Boston Tea Party, 29–30
Boycotts (colonial era), 29
Boylston, Zabdiel, 132–33
Braddock, Edward, 48
Bradford, William, 17, 18
Brent, Margaret, 16
British rule, 29–31
Brother Jonathan, 34
Burial customs, 136–37
Bush, George H.W., 77

C

Callender, James Thomson, 44
Camp, Walter, 149
Carlson, Chester, 98
Carnegie, Andrew, 80–81, 105
Cartwright, Alexander, 147
Carver, George Washington, 90
Castro, Fidel, 73
Chadwick, Cassie, 81
Cherry sisters, 156
Chicago, Great Fire of, 60–61
Child, Julia, 125

Chile, Lydia Maria, 152–53
China, 75
Chinese Exclusion Act, 59
Civil War, 54–56, 135, 143–44
Clark, William, 47
Clothing and fashion, 126–31
Cochrane, Josephine Garis, 97
Codman, Ogden Jr., 110
Cody, William Frederick "Wild Bill," 168–69
Cold War era, 71–77
Colton, Frank B., 99
Computers, 97–98, 103–5
Confederate states, 55
Constitutional Convention, 40–41
Continental Army, 34–38
Copy machines, 98
Cotton gin, 43
Crocker, Charles, 83
Cuba, 62–63, 73

D

Dale's Code, 15
Dance, 143, 144
Dawes, William, 31
Declaration of Independence, 33
The Decoration of Houses (Wharton, Codman), 110
Deere, John, 89
Delmonico's restaurant, 122
Depressions, economic, 66–67, 92, 94–95
Desegregation, 73
Dick and Jane readers, 118
Dishwashers, 97
Doubleday, Abner, 148
Dow Jones Industrial Stocks, 92
Dutch colonies, 25–26
Dyer, Mary, 21

E

Eckert, J. Presler, 103
Economy, 66–67, 91–95
Edison, Thomas, 100, 105
Education, 105, 118
Einstein, Isadore "Izzy," 66
Eisenhower, Dwight D., 71–72
Electoral College, 49–50

Emancipation Proclamation, 55
Embalming, 137
Emergency medicine, 135–36
Entertainment. See specific types
Environmental movements, 83, 137
Epidemics, 61
Epizootic, 134
"Exodusters," 58

F

Family life, 116–19
Farming, 23, 87–90, 92
Fashion, 126–31
Fauntleroy fashion fad, 127
The Federalist, 41
Ferguson, Patrick, 39
First Bank of the United States, 44–45
Food and restaurants, 120–25
Food rationing, 124
Football, 149–51
Ford, Henry, 82, 90, 105
Forrest, Edwin, 156–57
France, 27, 37
Franklin, Benjamin, 33, 37, 108
Free speech, 26–27
Frolics, 140–41
"Frontier thesis," 61–62

G

Gambling, 146
Games and sports, 146–51
Garrison, William Lloyd, 52
Gates, Bill, 104, 105
Gates, John, 89
Gaud, William, 90
Georgia, 24–25, 51
Gernsback, Hugo, 154
Gettysburg Address, 54
G.I. Bill, 111
Gibson Girls, 128
Gilded Age, 60–63, 122–23
The Gilded Age (Twain, Warner), 60
Glidden, Joseph F., 89
Goddard, Mary Katherine, 33
Goddard, Robert H., 102
Goodyear, Charles, 101
Gould, Jay, 82
Graham, Sylvester, 120–21

Granada, U.S. invasion of, 75
Great Depression, 66–67, 92
Guadalupe Hidalgo Treaty, 52–53

H

Hair permanents, 131
Hairstyles, 126
Hale, Sarah Josepha, 116
Hamilton, Alice, 134
Hamilton, Andrew, 26–27, 44–45
Harriman, Edward Henry, 83
Harrison, Benjamin, 50
"Harvey Girls," 123
Hawaii, 62
Hayes, Rutherford B., 18, 50, 57
Hearst, William Randolph, 62–63, 105
Heinz, Henry John, 123–24
Hemmings, Sally, 44
Hepburn, Katharine, 128
Highways, 48, 71–72
A History of . . . George Washington
   (Weems), 119
Hoboes, 96
Hollerith, Herman, 97–98
Holmes, Thomas, 137
Hopkins, Mark, 83
House and barn raisings, 141
Housing, 107–11
Houston, Charles Hamilton, 73
How the Other Half Lives (Riis), 118
Huntington, Collis P., 83
Hutchinson, Anne, 19
Hyde, Edward, 24

I

Illness and injury, 61, 99, 132–36
Income tax, 64
Indentured servants, 84
Industrialists, 79–83
Insanity defense, 115
Interior design, 110–11
Intolerable Acts, 30–31
Inventors, 43, 97–101
IT revolution, 103–5

J

Jackson, Andrew, 49, 50–51
Jamestown colony, 13–15, 23
Jefferson, Thomas, 33, 44, 47, 48–49
"Jim Crow" laws, 57

K

Kansas, 58
Kellogg, John Harvey, 121
Kennedy, John F., 104
King Philip's War, 19–20
King's Mountain, 39
Korean War, 136

L

Labor, 84–85
La Follette, Robert M. "Fighting Bob," 63
Land acquisition, 45–46, 51
Language, 26, 72, 96, 129, 153
Lawyers, 16, 18
Letterman, Jonathan, 135
Lewis, Meriwether, 47
The Liberator, 52
Library of Congress, 47
Life Among the Piutes
   (Winnemucca), 59
Liliuokalani (Queen of Hawaii), 62
Lillie, Gordon William "Pawnee Bill," 169
Limners, 24
Lincoln, Abraham, 53–54
Lindbergh, Charles A., 70
Literacy rates, 152
Lotteries, 146
Louisiana Purchase, 45
Lucas, Eliza, 87–88
Lumber trade, 15–16

M

Macready, William C., 156–57
Madison, Dolley, 48, 109
Mail-order brides, 117
"Manifest Destiny," 51
Manufacturing, 79
Marathon (1904), 149
Ma-re Mount settlers, 17–18
Marriage, 14–15, 21–22, 112–17
Marshall, Thurgood, 73

Mather, Cotton, 132–33
Matthews, John, 124–25
Mauchly, John, 103
May, Dorothy, 17
May Day, 109–10
Mayflower, 17
McCormick, Cyrus H., 89
Medical advances, 99, 132–36
Mencken, H. L., 65
"Mercer Girls," 117
Metacom ("King Philip"), 19–20
Military. See specific wars or
    operations
Minimum wage, 84–85
Monroe, Elizabeth Kortright, 49
Moon walk, 74–75
Morgan, J. P., 81
Morris, Robert, 38
Morton, Thomas, 17–18
Movies, 158–60
Muggs, J. Fred, 164
Muir, John, 83
Murder cases, 115
Museums, 166
Music and dance, 142–45

N

Nancy Drew books, 154
National symbols, emblems, 28
Natural disasters, 61
New Deal, 93
New York Stock Exchange (NYSE), 91
Nintendo, 151

O

Obama, Barack, 18, 77, 104
Obstetrics, 133
Occupational medicine, 134
Oglethorpe, James, 24–25
"OK," 153
O'Leary's cow, 60–61
Olympic games (1904), 148–49
Operation Little Vittles, 71
Operation Mongoose, 73
Operation Urgent Fury, 75
Oral contraceptives (the pill), 99
"Orphan trains," 117–18
Otis, Elisha, 100

P

Patent medicines, 133
Patterson, Elizabeth "Betsy," 114–15
Penn, William Jr., 22
Phillips, Irna, 162
"Ping pong diplomacy," 75
Pirate war, 46–47
Pitcher, Molly, 36
Pocahontas, 15
Poe, Edgar Allen, 153
Polio, 99, 135
Polk, James K., 52–53
Poor Richard's Almanac, 108
Post, Charles William, 121–22
Prescott, Samuel, 31
Presidents, U.S., 18, 49–50, 63, 68–69.
    See also specific presidents
Progressive reform movement, 63
Prohibition, 65–66
Pullman Strike, 85
Puritans, 16–22

Q

Quakers, 21, 22

R

Radio, 161–62
Railroads, 57–58, 82–83, 96
Rankin, Janette, 64–65
Reading and books, 47, 118, 152–54
Reconstruction era, 57–58
Reed, Walter, 135
Religion (colonial era), 16–22
Republican Party, 53
Restaurants, 122–25
Revere, Paul, 31
Revolutionary War, 31, 34–41
Riis, Jacob, 118
Roaring Twenties, 91
Rochambeau, Comte de, 38–39
Rock and roll, 144–45
Rockefeller, John D., 82, 105
Rolfe, John, 15
Roosevelt, Franklin D., 70, 93, 135
Roosevelt, Theodore, 149
Root, George Frederick, 143–44
Ross, Betsy, 35

S

Sabin, Albert, 99, 135
Salesmen, door-to-door, 85
Salk, Jonas, 99, 135
Salomon, Haym, 38
Saratoga, Battle of, 41
Scopes Monkey Trial, 65
Sears, 111
Sexual activity, 21–22, 99
Shakespeare, William, 14
Shipping, 80
Shopping, history of, 86
Singer, Isaac, 101
Sixties (1960s), 74
Slang terms, 26, 72, 96, 129, 153
Slater, Samuel, 79
Slavery, 43–44, 52
Smallpox, 132–33
Smith, Moe, 66
Soap operas, 161–62
Society of the Cincinnati, 39–40
Soda fountains, 124–25
Space exploration, 74–75, 102–3
Spanish-American War, 62–63, 135
Spencer-Churchill, Charles Richard John, 113–14
Sports, 147–51
Stanford, Leland, 83
Stockings, 130
Stratemeyer, Edward, 154
Supreme Court, 45, 73

T

Taverns, colonial, 32, 139–40
Taxi dancers, 144
Television, 162–64
The Tempest (Shakespeare), 14
Temple, Shirley, 129–30
Tenement life, 118
Tennessee, 55
Theater and film, 155–60
Thompson, Jeremiah, 80
Tightrope walkers, 168
Tobacco, 14–15, 23, 84, 87, 97, 108–9
Tonkin Gulf Resolution, 76
"Trail of Tears," 51
Treasury, U.S., 44–45
Tripoli, 46–47

Trist, Nicholas P., 52–53
Trumbo, Dalton, 159
Turner, Jackson, 61–62
Twain, Mark, 60

U

U.S. Capitol Building, 77

V

Vanderbilt, Consuelo, 113–14
Vanderbilt, Cornelius, 82, 105
Van Lew, Elizabeth "Crazy Bet," 56
Victory gardens, 124
Video games, 151
Vietnam Veterans Memorial wall, 76
Vietnam War, 74, 76, 136

W

War of Jenkins's Ear, 25
Washington, George, 21, 34, 40, 41, 43, 48, 107, 119
Weems, Mason Locke, 119
Weetamo, 20
Westinghouse, George, 101
Wharton, Edith, 110–11
Whitney, Eli, 43
Whittier, John Greenleaf, 57
Williams, Roger, 17
Winnemucca, Sarah, 59
Women, 14–15, 16, 36, 64–65, 133
Works Progress Administration (WPA), 93
World War I, 67, 136
World War II, 67–70, 111, 124, 136
World Wide Web, 105

Y

"Yankee," 26
Yellow journalism, 62–63, 64
Yeltsin, Boris, 77
Yorktown, Battle of, 41

Z

Zenger, John Peter, 26–27

About the Authors

Fred DuBose, a native Texan, is a writer, editor, and book developer based in New York City. He served as an editorial director of Reader's Digest Illustrated Reference Books and is the author of an eclectic collection of books with subjects as varied as tomatoes, grandparents, cooking, and wine.

Martha Hailey, a journalist who has lived and worked in Belgium and Australia, is a former film critic and advertising executive. Now living in her native Tennessee, she is the author of a number of books, including an Edgar-nominated critical history of women writers of detective fiction.

Enjoy These Other Reader's Digest Best-Sellers

Featuring all the memory-jogging tips you'll ever need to know, this fun little book will help you recall hundreds of important facts using simple, easy-to-remember mnemonics from your school days.

$14.95 hardcover
ISBN 978–0–7621–0917–3

Make learning fun again with these light-hearted pages that are packed with important theories, phrases, and those long-forgotten "rules" you once learned in school.

$14.95 hardcover
ISBN 978–0–7621–0995–1

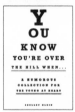

This laugh-out-loud collection of heartwarming jokes, quips, and truisms about the joys of aging will keep you entertained for hours.

$14.95 hardcover
ISBN 978–1–60652–025–3

Confused about when to use "its" or "it's" or the correct spelling of "principal" or "principle"? Avoid language pitfalls and let this entertaining and practical guide improve both your speaking and writing skills.

$14.95 hardcover
ISBN 978–1–60652–026–0

Fun and fascinating facts and quips about authors and books—from the classics to contemporary literature. A book that is sure to delight bookworms and trivia buffs.

$14.95 hardcover
ISBN 978–1–60652–034–5

Reader's Digest books can be purchased through retail and online bookstores.
In the United States books are distributed by Penguin Group (USA), Inc.
For more information or to order books, call 1-800-788-6262.